REVELATION
THE BIBLE ENDING EXPLAINED

by
Eddie Turner

This book is dedicated to
Durl H. Schultz.

I was young. And you showed me the way I should go.

I am old now. And I have not departed from it, "pardner."

Copyright © 2025 by Eddie Turner

ISBN 978-1-7321714-6-6

Selections of Scripture used in this book are borrowed from the NASB, NIV and ESV translations of the Holy Bible.

More information about books by Eddie Turner
can be found at dayofredemption.org.

All rights reserved. No part of this book may be reproduced in any form without the written permission of the author except in the case of brief quotations for the purposes of reviewing or promoting.

I, Jesus, have sent my angel to give you this testimony for the churches.

REVELATION 22:16

CONTENTS

PAGE 1	THIRTY MINUTES
PAGE 7	VISIONS
PAGE 17	EPOCHS
PAGE 29	MISCONCEPTIONS
PAGE 45	RAPTURE
PAGE 55	THE CAST
PAGE 65	REVELATION 1 & 2
PAGE 71	REVELATION 3 & 4
PAGE 77	REVELATION 5 & 6

PAGE **83**	**REVELATION 7 & 8**
PAGE **89**	**REVELATION 9 & 10**
PAGE **95**	**REVELATION 11 & 12**
PAGE **103**	**REVELATION 13 & 14**
PAGE **109**	**REVELATION 15 & 16**
PAGE **113**	**REVELATION 17 & 18**
PAGE **119**	**REVELATION 19 & 20**
PAGE **125**	**REVELATION 21 & 22**
PAGE **131**	**REFLECTION**

THIRTY MINUTES

When I was younger, my friends and I would go to the movies at a multiplex much like the ones we have today. Often, when a movie ended, we would hang out in the lobby for a bit, maybe play an arcade game or two, and then have a seat in another auditorium to watch a second movie that we hadn't paid to see. And we usually saw other people doing this too. In fact, the theater was so well known for this activity that its staff had to know this was going on. But we never saw anyone get kicked out. The tickets didn't include seat numbers, and no one checked them anyway. When you were in, you were in.

One afternoon, while attending one of these "double features," my best friend and I learned that it would be an hour before the second movie we wanted to see began. There were other options, but they were either movies we'd already seen or just didn't want to see. So, we decided to watch what was left of the desired movie in progress, which was about thirty minutes.

When it was over, we heard a lot of chatter about the film as people left their seats. Apparently, the movie was really good. So, I decided to join one of the conversations to determine if I wanted to come back and watch it from the beginning. And I decided against it after getting an earful of spoilers from people who didn't know I'd only caught the tail end. But they knew something was up when I couldn't comment on the scenes that they were all raving about. Needless to say, I'd have no business writing a review of that film if I were a movie critic.

Today, I am a father and a husband who still enjoys going to the movies. I pay for all of them, by the way. I'm also an author with three books, under my belt, one of which took me nine years to get on a bookshelf. That book is "a comprehensive look at our future from day one of the tribulation period to the end of our first thousand years in God's presence," according to the summary I wrote for the back cover. It's called *Antichrist: The Biblical End of Days*—my magnum opus. And it was during those years of study and preparation that I learned there's more information in the Bible about the end times than I had ever been taught. WAY more. I even found clear answers to questions that I was told could not be answered until we were in heaven. Yet there they were, written in black and red. And when I shared my research with my pastor at the time, he became baffled over how he and the professors at the theological seminary he attended had not connected the dots that I had. As pleased as I was to hear this from a man I held in such high regard, I began to feel a bit unsure of myself. I mean, it wasn't just him and a few professors who didn't see what I saw. It was everyone who'd ever taught me anything about the Bible.

And so, in an effort to ease this growing concern of mine, I embarked on a personal mission to find others whose understanding of the end times mirrored my own. But it wasn't long before God's Spirit showed me that I was essentially seeking human affirmation of His wisdom. So, I stopped looking, but not before seeing how teachers, pastors, and even theologians had presented their understanding of Revelation as if they had only watched the last thirty minutes of a movie. And by movie, I mean the Bible. I'm not suggesting that none of these people had read the Bible before. I'm sure they had. But they were treating this book as if it were the *entire* movie, using their own ideas to fill in gaps that books like Ezekiel, Jeremiah, and Daniel had already filled in. This also explained why I hadn't been able to pinpoint some of the more popular teachings about the end times within the pages of the Bible. I thought I was just dumb or something. So, this was a relief.

Just as there are teachers with a particular passion for topics like creation, discipleship, and archeology, God has turned my heart toward *eschatology*, which is the study of humanity's last days on earth and life thereafter. It represents a new beginning in the presence of our Lord and Savior, Jesus Christ. It's also a topic that the world has made into a horror movie instead of the love story that it is. I aim to fix that. And so, because Revelation is not an ideal starting point for a study of the last days, I've prepared some discussions and selected portions of Scripture that I believe will serve as prerequisites, or things you need to know before you begin studying.

Because our focus will be mainly on this one book, I will not cover every end-times event that we learn about outside of Revelation. You can read my other book if you'd like a broader scope of this topic. The purpose of *this* book is to refresh your memory of the rest of the movie and point out parts of the story that you might have missed or may not have been looking for.

There are also some ground rules specific to studying Revelation that we'll go over. Knowing how people who don't follow them tend to go off in strange directions, I'd say they're pretty important. Anyway, once you're up to speed, I'll walk you through Revelation chapter by chapter. We might even have some laughs along the way, depending upon your tolerance for cheesy dad jokes. Much like Moses and his tablets, I've been known to throw down a few. Oh, one last thing. I know I've only written these few paragraphs, but I can't help wondering how many pages this book will end up having. So, if you think about it when you get to the end, come back here and let me know. I'd appreciate it.

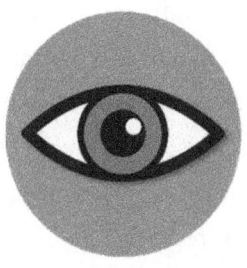

VISIONS

In the previous chapter, I emphasized how watching only the last part of a movie will never allow you to understand the entire story. Ironically, we're about to begin a close look at the last part of the Bible where John, the youngest of the disciples, was essentially watching a movie. Beginning with the fourth chapter of Revelation, John's perspective shifts from an actual visit with Jesus to a virtual encounter, much like a lucid dream. The Bible refers to this experience as a "vision," and John is not the first to have one. If you recall, Daniel also had one of these visions. And both of their experiences were to inform these men about the time of the end. In John's vision, he saw a giant angel, a talking bird, a dragon with horns, and other creatures one might expect to see in a fantasy movie. As vivid as his descriptions may be, the understanding that his first-century mind would not have allowed him to identify things of the future is very common.

Today, many believe that John didn't actually see what he said he did. Some have even taken it upon themselves to name what he may have seen instead. For example, the armored locust-like demons John wrote about are reckoned to have been military attack helicopters or fighter jets. And his account of a giant falling star has been reimagined as a nuclear missile. Though certainly interesting, there's a sizable conflict with this view—visions didn't involve time travel.

Contrary to what many have concluded, there's no evidence that points to John having been brought into the future to witness events as they unfold in real time. Rather, this entire encounter was a surreal experience that God used to inform him of events that will happen later. This included a view of God's throne room, complete with the sights and sounds that one would see and hear if they were actually there. John, however, was *not* there. And he was fully aware that this was purely a spiritual encounter, and even said so at the beginning of the fourth chapter and twice more before the book concludes. But he recalled this entire affair as though he had lived through it.

THE THEATER

One of the most popular virtual reality apps available today allows users to customize their own movie theater experience. I tried out the demo a few months ago using my son's VR headset, and I was truly amazed. I could choose colors for the walls and flooring, select types of lighting, adjust the rise of the stadium seating, and even make changes to the speaker configuration that actually impacted the sound. I was even able to adjust the brightness and color levels of the movie screen separately, which was an awesome feature. Finally, as the movie played, I could gaze around the theater just as I can inside a real one, and even do some mid-move redecorating if I wanted to.

Although this experience felt real, my immersion was somewhat limited. Not only was I sitting in an office chair instead of one of the comfy recliners I added, everyday household noises were hard to tune out. Trust me—hearing a cat meow inside a movie theater is very odd indeed. There was also an ad on the seat in front of me because I hadn't paid to unlock the full version of the app. I thought having a bucket of popcorn in my lap might help matters. But my son reminded me that, while wearing the headset, I wouldn't be able to see the popcorn… or my lap for that matter. I was an invisible man in a chair. When I was done, I decided that the best way to use this app required wearing the headset while sitting in an actual movie theater. I know. Purpose defeated. But this was still the coolest movie experience I've ever had at home. And I plan to revisit it at some point. Now, let's kick this up a notch.

When you're done marveling over what total nerds my family must be, take a moment and reflect on the last vacation you took. Mine was at Universal Studios in Orlando. It's only been a month since I was there, and I can still taste the butter beer I had in the Harry Potter-themed area after getting off of the greatest thrill ride I'd ever experienced. It was the one beneath Hogwarts Castle in case you're curious. I also recall the songs that played during a parade and how my feet ached after walking around in the hot sun all day. But what if I never actually went on this trip? Would I be able to have such vivid memories that all five of my senses affirm if I never left the house? The answer is no, obviously. But for John, his recollection of tastes, sounds, and intense emotional reactions to the things he saw and even touched strongly suggests that this is what happened. He didn't just wake from a dream. He possessed a genuine memory of a trip he never took. Mind blown? Mine certainly is. Just remember that it was God who initiated all this. And He's in the mind-blowing business.

THE PRESENTATION

Now, let's look at how this virtual scenario plays out in Revelation. As his vision began, John found himself inside God's throne room, which he described in great detail. In addition to the splendor of God's glory, he saw angels, a number of beings who served as elders, and even some fantastical-looking creatures who continually offered their praises to God. And it was in this virtual surrounding that a series of moving images was presented to John, each image preceded by either an announcement or an action within the throne room. While some images were merely symbolic of future events, other images depicted dramatizations of the events themselves. And just like in Daniel's vision, there was an angel present to explain what John was seeing so he wouldn't wake up thinking that army helicopters were bugs.

Now, the first set of images were triggered by Jesus breaking the seals on a scroll that God had given him. When the first seal was broken, the first of four riders on horseback was summoned to appear before John. This image was attributed to victory that will result in peace on the earth. And when Jesus broke the second seal, the second rider that appeared was symbolic of the war that would put an end to that peace. John did not see the world at peace, nor did he see a war, of course. He only saw images that represented these events. As for the goings-on inside the throne room, it's entirely possible they were performed solely for the purpose of this vision. Does this mean that Jesus won't be breaking seals to trigger these events in the future? I believe it does. While focusing on the explanations rather than the visuals may be our greatest asset, I know some of you are movie-goers like me. So, I've outlined a few of these repeating sequences to help you identify the nature of each step.

Example 1

- Jesus breaking a seal *(virtual, demonstrative)*
- The rider on a white horse *(virtual, symbolic)*
- Victory/peace on the earth *(spoken, real-world future event)*

Example 2

- An angel pours out a golden bowl *(virtual, demonstrative)*
- John sees that a plague ensues *(dramatization, demonstrative)*
- The plague *(real-world future event)*

Example 3

- An angel blows a trumpet *(virtual, demonstrative)*
- John sees that blood and hail ensue *(dramatization, demonstrative)*
- The blood and hail *(real-world future event)*

Whenever an image lacks a sufficient explanation, the visual in question may have been introduced and explained earlier in the Bible. Here's an example.

And the beast which I saw was like a leopard, and his feet were like those of a bear, and his mouth like the mouth of a lion. And the dragon gave him his power and his throne and great authority.

Revelation 13:2

In this verse, the lion, the leopard, and the bear were seen together in Daniel's vision about the time of the end. These images were used to paint a picture of how progress over time will lead to growing hostility toward Israel. And the beast (the Antichrist) is said to emulate the ferociousness in all three of these animals combined. So, while the images that Daniel and John saw included features of these animals, I feel confident that this is not how the Antichrist will appear to the world when he's a beast. I could say, "We'll just have to wait and see," but I'm not planning on being around to confirm a lot of this stuff. I hope you aren't either.

IMPRISONED

While John's mind and spirit were on vacation, his body was on a *stay*-cation on an island called Patmos. According to historians, this island served as a prison camp for those whose crimes warranted their exile from society. There's also evidence that John was up in age when he was placed there. Today, Patmos can be seen on a map just off of Turkey's westernmost shoreline.

As for the details surrounding his imprisonment, we're only told that his crime involved proclaiming the gospel. There is, however, an extra-biblical resource claiming John was sentenced after being labeled a witch for having climbed out of a vat of boiling tar completely unscathed. This information, however, is questionable at best. So, we can treat it as a work of fiction where any similarity to actual events or persons, living or dead, is purely *intentional*.

In addition to being the great physician, God is the great *mathematician*. I call Him that anyway. In addition to telling us what's going to happen in the future, God makes a valiant effort to inform us *when* these things will occur. And He does this with numbers that serve as the framework for the times that lie ahead. In the next chapter, we'll examine some of these numbers that help us visualize God's timeline of end-times events. Speaking of which, you may have noticed that I didn't include chapter numbers in this book. Knowing that my chapter titles would eventually include numbers, I decided not to cram an extra one in there. I usually just reference book chapters by their content anyway. In the novel I'm currently reading, I'm in the chapter where that girl with the hair and the guy in that shirt went to that place and did the stuff that made all those things happen. Such a great book! I highly recommend it.

THE TOUR

Before we move on, let's talk about what I've chosen to refer to as a *walkthrough* of Revelation. While the idea of writing a full commentary is certainly interesting, I've not felt led to take on a project of that scope. But I have indeed been called to teach. And so, as a teacher, I'll be presenting Revelation the same way I have in classroom settings. This involves presenting selections of its text and discussing key points that lend themselves to a greater understanding of the book and its place among the 65 books of the Bible that precede it. Because we're not in a classroom setting, I can't see who has their Bible and who doesn't. But I do urge you to follow along in yours once we begin. If you're on a plane and don't have room for two books, I'll let it slide this time.

Revelation has provided me with new and thought-provoking experiences each time I've studied it. It's even prompted me to break out in worship all by myself. With that said, if you take only one thing away from our time together, let it be what I'm about to share. One's motive for studying God's Word should always be the desire to draw closer to Him. Do not set out to prove anyone wrong or correct those whose understanding of the Bible is different from your own. While this book certainly provides fuel for this activity, my primary motivation for writing it is to share what

God has revealed to me as I continue to seek a deeper relationship with Him. When our motives are fueled by anything else, we may as well be blind. Only when we pursue God's grace and pray for His wisdom may we be given ears to hear and eyes to see.

EPOCHS

Let's now discuss the significance of the various time periods associated with the end of days, which make up the infamous seven years known as the tribulation period. And we'll begin by focusing our attention on Israel, which is what those seven years are all about.

So when they had come together, they were asking Him, saying, "Lord, is it at this time You are restoring the kingdom to Israel?" He said to them, "It is not for you to know times or epochs which the Father has fixed by His own authority; but you will receive power when the Holy Spirit has come upon you; and you shall be My witnesses both in Jerusalem, and in all Judea and Samaria, and even to the remotest part of the earth."

Acts 1:6-8

There's a lot to unpack in these verses, starting with what Jesus told his disciples was prohibited.

This involved having knowledge of *epochs*, which are periods of time that are significant to one event or another. And the epoch Jesus' disciple asked about was off limits. This verse is often used to discourage people like me from using spreadsheets to chart timelines in the Bible. Jesus, however, only outlawed the time periods that are known only to God, making them impossible for us to analyze anyway. As for the rest of them, I conclude that we're free to go bonkers with the oodles of days, weeks, and years that are tied to numbers in Scripture.

We also see a reference to the 144,000 Jews that Revelation speaks of. These are men and women who will be around after the rapture to continue spreading the gospel to those left behind. And numbers help us paint this picture. We'll revisit this group later on. Now, let's focus on what is called the Restoration of Israel, an event that, despite having similar wording, is not mentioned in that verse. To be honest, I have no clue what that disciple was asking about. But I know it's something different because we know all about this epoch—all 70 of them.

70 WEEKS

Seventy weeks have been decreed for your people and your holy city, to finish the wrongdoing, to make an end of sin, to make atonement for guilt, to bring in

everlasting righteousness, to seal up vision and prophecy, and to anoint the Most Holy Place.

Daniel 9:24

In the eleventh chapter of Romans, we are told that "all Israel" will be saved at the time of the end. While there are differing opinions about what "all" means in this text, I'm gonna to go out on a limb and say that it doesn't mean *some*. And there's a refining process that God's chosen will undergo in order to be saved, or *restored* to Him. According to Daniel's angelic assistant during his vision, it's a three-step program that will unfold over the course of seventy weeks. Each "week," however, is actually seven years. And these weeks are divided into three groups: 7 weeks (49 years), 62 weeks (434 years), and 1 week (7 years). If we do the math, we'll see that there's a grand total of 490 years. Bear with me, folks. This does get interesting.

According to Daniel, the first group of 7 weeks (49 years) began when a decree was made to rebuild Jerusalem. This occurred around 557 BC after the people of Israel had spent years in captivity by the Babylonians. And the next group of 62 weeks (434 years) concluded when Jesus was born. This assures us that there was a gap of 70+ years between these two groups. There's also a gap of time between the end of the 62 weeks and the beginning of the final 1 week.

And that gap is expanding every day because that last week hasn't happened yet. This is the seven-year period that plays out in Revelation. So, while these epochs do occur in sequence, they aren't bumped right up next to each other. Crazy as it may seem, I may be in the minority when it comes to this understanding.

If there's one thing I've learned as a Bible teacher, it's that minds tend to wander off when a lesson turns into a math class. So, if you only mildly grasped the info in the last two paragraphs, you may not recognize the train wrecks that occur when one insists that these three epochs must occur back-to-back. And I do mean wrecks (plural) because there are two scenarios to consider. The first one agrees that the first 7-week period started when it actually did. But removing the time gaps pulls the next two periods into the past, causing everything we're learning about in Revelation to have already happened. On the flip side, there's the view that the final week occurs in the future, with the other two periods immediately preceding it. The problem here is that the second group concludes with the Nativity. So, Jesus' birth would need to happen twice if this were accurate. Kind of gives a new meaning to the words, born again! Anyway, you get the picture. I just felt it was important to go over this because it's not uncommon that this understanding is shared without realizing the ramifications.

So, the Bible's presentation of these 70 weeks is pivotal to our understanding what the tribulation period is all about. While this final week occurs toward the end of the timeline, it's still part of an initiative that began a long, long time ago. Yes, it's killing me that I can't include "in a galaxy far, far away."

SIX-DAY WAR

Yet another epoch concerning Israel consists of only six days. Commonly referred to as the Six-Day War, this event resulted in the Israelites reclaiming their promised land in 1967 after being scattered among the nations for their persistent disobedience to God.

"I will gather you from the peoples and assemble you from the countries among which you have been scattered, and I will give you the land of Israel."
Ezekiel 11:17

In this section, I'll attempt to bring you up to speed on the current state of Israel. In order to get there, we'll need to jump back in time even further to 1947, when a remnant of the Jews occupied Israel along with people from the Arab nations. Seeing that the two groups weren't playing nice with each other, the United Nations stepped in and proposed that the land be divided into two states—Israel and Palestine. This was a temporary solution that the UN hoped would put an end to the Arab-Israeli feuds. Boy, were they wrong. A year later, when this arrangement expired, Jewish leaders declared the establishment of the State of Israel without recognizing the Palestinian border. And this further ticked off the Arabs, whose armies attacked the Israelis the following day.

When the dust settled, the two groups were separated once again. The Arabs were given the Gaza Strip and the Israelis the West Bank—two areas that can be seen on any modern map. Israel, however, began expanding its occupation into areas beyond the West Bank. And the lack of any official borders resulted in the Israelis settling in parts of Egypt, Jordan, and Lebanon, who offered to establish borders for Israel if they would get their people out of their countries. Israel complied, and the borders were set. These borders, however, only established the areas that belonged to these three countries rather than what belonged to Israel.

While there are many nations that recognize the Jewish state of Israel, many still reject its . . . officialness. It's a word. I checked. And the majority of countries that reject Israel's right to exist are right along its borders. So, the whole "love thy neighbor" commandment never really gained traction over there, I guess. Today, the Israeli government continues to expand its occupation by building homes and mega apartment complexes in contested areas. Coupled with its ongoing attacks on Gaza, these moves are only adding fuel to this raging fire that is the Middle Eastern Conflict. Now, about that temple…

THIRD TEMPLE

If you've read through Revelation, you're probably aware of the text that describes the presence of a Jewish temple in Jerusalem. You may also be aware that there's not one there right now. There are, however, big plans for its construction in place as you read this. And those plans include the temple being built where the last one stood before it was destroyed ages ago. This site is called the Temple Mount. You know, because it's where the temple was mounted. Duh! So, if the Temple Mount is in Jerusalem and Jerusalem is in Israel, why aren't they already building it? Good question! This has to do with another one of those feuds between the Israelis and the Arabs. Cue another flashback sequence.

Back in 2010, Israel was tipped off about a fleet of ships full of pro-Hamas activists whose intention was to break through the Israeli Defense Force (IDF) military blockade to avoid inspection. And when they did this, IDF soldiers boarded the ships and forced them to dock. While five of the ships were compliant, those who manned a sixth vessel refused to surrender.

And, as some of you may recall hearing on the news, all hell broke loose in an exchange of gunfire that left nine activists dead and many more wounded. At this, the UN reprised its role as kindergarten teacher and made Israel apologize by handing over the management of the Temple Mount to an Islamic organization, which in turn banned all Jews from utilizing the site as a place of prayer. And, of course, they aren't allowed to build anything there either—yet.

1,000 YEARS

This is the last epoch we'll examine in this chapter, and it appears to have no significance to Israel. Rather, the events that round out this time period apply to those who will have waited too long to surrender to Jesus. On the day of the rapture, the earth will be wiped clean of every saved soul whose name is written in the book of life. These will be rewarded with eternal life. But there will indeed be many more who become saved after the rapture. Their surrender will occur in the midst of the unimaginable horror with which God will smite the earth following our rescue. These must either be killed for their faith in Christ or survive with their testimony, avoiding the plagues and any entanglement with the Antichrist. While each of these 'tribulation saints' will be present on the new earth, their reward will be limited to one thousand years.

And I saw the souls of those who had been beheaded because of their testimony of Jesus and because of the word of God, and those who had not worshiped the beast or his image, and had not received the mark on their foreheads and on their hands; and they came to life and reigned with Christ for a thousand years.

Revelation 20:4

If this is new to you, you're not alone. Not by a long shot. I mean, no church I've ever attended has taught this as far as I'm aware, and I've not heard a sermon about it elsewhere—ever. But this is indeed a truth that Revelation assures us of multiple times. So, let's take a closer look at what the Bible teaches us.

When the thousand years are completed, Satan will be released from his prison, and will come out to deceive the nations which are at the four corners of the earth.

And they came up on the broad plain of the earth and surrounded the camp of the saints and the beloved city, and fire came down from heaven and devoured them.

Revelation 20:7, 9

Hopefully, most of you are familiar with this text. Despite its many interpretations that place this event on our current earth, the reaction to this deception involves access to the great city on the *new* earth, which raptured saints will be granted, and tribulation saints will be denied. We'll examine what causes people to understand this differently in the next chapter. As for the city being off-limits, this is one of multiple restrictions that God will impose upon these latecomers. And it's the one restriction Satan will use to turn them all against Jesus in an act of defiance that will result in their destruction at the end of the thousand years. Until that time, God will provide for them according to their needs—needs that raptured saints will not possess.

I will give to the one who thirsts from the spring of the water of life without cost.
Revelation 21:6

While this reward/life extension is specific to the tribulation saints, Isaiah's book informs us that these will not live for the full thousand years. Rather, they will die around the age of 100 and their children will succeed them. Just as a whole new generation of Israelites entered the Promised Land, Satan will tempt a generation born on the new earth who never knew life on our old one.

No longer will there be in it an infant who lives but a few days, or an old man who does not live out his

days. For the youth will die at the age of one hundred and the one who does not reach the age of one hundred will be thought accursed.

They will not labor in vain, or bear children for calamity. For they are the offspring of those blessed by the Lord, and their descendants with them.

Isaiah 65:20, 23

Next, we read about the judgment of "the dead," which refers to the deceased souls whose names are not written in the book of life. This includes the tribulation saints as well as the generations of their offspring who'll either have died at age 100 or whose lives God will end just prior to this day. Once again, their names will not be written in the book. We know this because only those whose names were indeed written in the book will be resurrected and rescued at the time of the rapture, leaving behind those who will be killed for their testimony, given white robes, and who will be residents on the new earth during the thousand years.

This assures us that, on the new earth, there will be two groups; the first of which will possess glorified bodies which are incapable of sin and will never die. The second group will be capable of sin, require food and water, give birth to children, and succumb to deception as well as death. So, might these possess normal human bodies? It sure sounds like it.

Speaking of deception, there are numerous things that people believe about the end times that are not mentioned in Revelation or anywhere else in the Bible. Embracing these ideas, however, may not all be the result of malicious intent. They won't rob us of our salvation either. But there does appear to be some worldly influences at play here that can impact one's understanding of God's character. So, unless I get my numberless chapters mixed up, this will be the topic of our next discussion. While I'm quite pleased at how this chapter turned out, writing it has only made me realize how hard it is to keep eschatological time periods all in one place. So, you can expect more biblical number crunching in the pages ahead. Don't everybody get all excited at once.

MISCONCEPTIONS

In this chapter, I'll share with you some questionable ideas that people famously tie to various passages within Revelation. Some may be the result of simple misunderstandings. And yet others seem to involve a bit of creative effort to suppose that the Bible describes such things. When audiences who embrace these ideas are limited to small pockets of people here and there, finding the culprit may not be too difficult. When entire denominations of Bible readers are involved, however, pinpointing the origin of the misinformation may be downright impossible. So, instead of learning what happened, we're often limited to knowing how it *can* happen. Here's one scenario that fits the bill.

When Jesus appeared to his disciples after he was crucified, he assured them that he was not a ghost. This is recorded in the 24th chapter of Luke's book. So, did any of these men actually believe in ghosts? It's hard to say. But they definitely knew what one was.

And Jesus used this word to assure them that he was the opposite of what they might have mistaken him for, given their knowledge of his death, and given Jesus' knowledge of them calling him a ghost when he was walking on water. Now, did Jesus affirm the existence of ghosts by saying this? No, he didn't. But if you were to become adamant that he did, imagine the numerous other verses you'd have to skew in order to argue your case. This would be like forcing a puzzle piece into a space where it doesn't fit. If you've ever done this, you know that it's not possible to do it with just one piece. You have to force many adjacent puzzle pieces into place as well, resulting in an image distorted by a big lump in the middle. While this distortion should be obvious, it may not be so obvious if this is how the puzzle was presented to you initially, and by someone whose puzzle-solving ability you fully trusted.

Before we move on, I want to stress that I have no desire to belittle anyone whose understanding of the Bible may include these ideas or any of the others I've made examples of in this book. I am equally guilty of not questioning things that sounded reasonable enough when they were presented to me. I'm simply following God's lead in presenting these concepts which I have become increasingly aware of over the years. Because the Bible claims to be useful for correction as well as teaching, I feel confident that I may use it for both of these purposes in my books. Again, these errors may not be salvation-breakers. But if exposing them brings us only a tiny bit closer to the truth, I say we go all in. Are you with me? Great. Let's begin.

BLOOD MOONS

In the same way a solar eclipse stirs people to report when Jesus is coming back on YouTube, the appearance of a *blood moon* tends to spark some prophetic frenzies. With little effort, you can find books and documentaries about how these occurrences will have great significance in the end times. A blood moon is attributed to a lunar eclipse when the sun's light is blocked by the earth, giving the moon a dull reddish-orange glow. It may also appear to be quite large, much like a harvest moon. While I haven't detected any such tie-ins to these blood moons in Revelation, there is indeed a verse about the moon turning red. This is the direct result of what God is going to do to the sun. This will also be a one-time event rather than something that has been happening in cycles for ages.

I looked when He broke the sixth seal, and there was a great earthquake; and the sun became black as sackcloth made of hair, and the whole moon became like blood.

Revelation 6:12

In the book of Acts, Jesus tells us about "wonders" that may be seen in the heavens as the end draws near. Rather than stationary objects in the sky, these phenomena consist of things falling from it—things like fire, giant stones of hail, and even the stars.

And I will grant wonders in the sky above and signs on the earth below; blood, and fire, and vapor of smoke.

Acts 2:19

And so, while there will indeed be a blood-red moon during these events, I feel confident that it is one that nobody has ever seen before. And I'm even more certain that none of us will want to be on the earth to see it when it happens.

INSERTING AMERICA

Knowing that my books have made their way across the world is pretty exciting. And it's prompted me to try and keep things on a universal level. But I have indeed shared some things specific to life in the United States. After all, that's where I live. And I've only encountered Americans who believe that Revelation is all about our country. But there may be those in Croatia, for example, who share this understanding. Of course, I'm referring to Croatians who believe Revelation is focused on Croatia. But they may also think it's all about the USA, for all I know. Anyway, this belief system has a name. It's called *Christian Nationalism*. Here are some actual examples of this mindset naming the United States as being central to the achievement of God's will. If you live in Israel, you get a free pass from this discussion.

> **The death of the two witnesses (Rev 11:7-8)** is believed to be a symbolic reference to the destruction of the twin towers of the World Trade Center in New York City.
>
> **The beast coming out of the sea (Rev 13:1)** is regarded as a reference to the USA, as its population derived from the nations that many attribute to the four beasts we learn about in Daniel.
>
> **The two horns of the second beast (Rev 13:11)** are said to point to the United States' two-party political system.
>
> **The great eagle (Rev. 8:13)** is believed to be the United States warning the rest of the world that God's wrath is coming.

What's crazy is the amount of work that goes into some of these wild claims. I once watched a guy go on for nearly an hour, weaving all kinds of intricate details into the Bible to support what amounted to a conspiracy theory involving the Illuminati. Some people are even convinced that the absence of the USA in the Bible is due to a great spiritual awakening or revival that will result in the exclusion of our people from God's wrath during terrible times ahead. In other words, Americans have a rapture guarantee. So, whether for good or for bad, the desire for the USA to take center stage within the many end-times prophecies is out there. I do recognize that referring to these as misconceptions is iffy. But they do involve concepts. And these concepts are definitely amiss.

ONE-WORLD RELIGION

This idea stems from the actions of a male figure the Bible refers to as the *false prophet*. In Revelation, we read of this man's affiliation with a church or religious institution that will have been around since Jesus' day and whose influence spans the globe. In an act that appears to be driven by cowardice, the false prophet will take cover behind the Antichrist's intimidation as he addresses people all over the world who missed the rapture, many for having followed his church's false teaching. And the speech he delivers will urge the earth's remaining inhabitants to worship and surrender their lives to the beast.

For whatever reason, the word *ecumenism* seems to follow this portion of Scripture. This term refers to a movement toward the uniting of multiple Christian denominations to form a single church. Some claim that this movement will be prevalent in the days leading up to the rapture, while others attribute it to this coerced surrender to the beast's authority. Any way you slice it, no portion of Scripture should lead us to believe that this false prophet's cowardly plea will result in any kind of organized religion. And I have encountered no text in the Bible that suggests this dissolving of denominational divides will be a thing as the end draws near.

UNIVERSAL CURRENCY

Talk of a one-world currency often accompanies discussions about the ecumenical church. While this topic is not nearly as far-fetched, it's merely a conclusion that can be reached if we allow our minds to wander a bit too far from the facts. And it too derives from the false prophet's speech to a broken world that will have become a dangerous place to live. In order to mold selling one's soul to Satan into an attractive package, the false prophet will toss in the perk of being able to once again buy and sell goods. This gives us a clue to just how bad things will have gotten after the rapture.

I picture cities whose looted stores and markets may halt any effort to replenish their shelves by farmers and manufacturers. And if the riots we've seen in our day are any indication, having money tucked away in a society without order may be useless. Anyway, I'm sure you can add your own imagery of a world fighting for survival after a portion of the world's population disappears. Hopefully, it won't come from that Nicolas Cage movie. I heard it was pretty bad.

While there may indeed be a single currency under the Antichrist's rule, I can't envision the level of organization that would be needed to develop a new money system, much less distribute it worldwide. But those who take the false prophet up on his offer may indeed be using a single currency. As for the type, I imagine that would be determined by the location of this evil operation, if those who submit are even required to migrate there. If they aren't, people might be using the same currency they're using now. Access to money, however, may be stunted along with opportunities to spend it if banks suffer the way I imagine stores will. Anyway, that's about as far as I can speculate on this matter.

OUT OF ORDER

A major stumbling block for people who study Revelation is the idea that the book is an account of purely chronological events. This is a *preconception* that many people have before they begin studying. As a result, everything they read must fit within that bubble. When a verse challenges this mindset, the reader is faced with a dilemma. He or she can either break out of that bubble or grab a concept like time travel and pull it inside with them. Much like the insistence that Israel's 70 weeks are consecutive, approaching Revelation in this manner has classically prompted people to reach some "interesting" conclusions.

For instance, because John shared information about events during the thousand-year period *before* he described seeing the new earth, many believe that we must all return to this earth for a thousand years before following Jesus to the new one. I used the word 'many,' but there are millions of people who ascribe to this. Commonly referred to as the 'Millennial Kingdom,' this idea fails to take into account the earth's destruction before the thousand years begin. It also places the great city, New Jerusalem on both the new earth *and* our old one. So, this chronological preconception is responsible for oodles of misconceptions. From regarding events that may only happen once as occurring multiple times to confusing the tribulation saints with the raptured ones, many who study Revelation just seem to plow through the brick walls this mindset creates.

When I was in college, I plowed through these same walls until I finally crashed into one. I just couldn't bring myself to believe that the Bible described what it didn't. And I couldn't fathom how anyone else could. And yet people did. This is what sparked that feeling of dumbness that I mentioned in the first chapter. Because my theology professor shared this preconception, I hadn't yet considered that the book might not be presented in a linear fashion the way other books were. So, my only option was to grit my teeth and keep on truckin'. Years later, and for an entirely different reason, I was led to discard everything I knew about Revelation and allow only the text and God's Spirit to guide me through it. And when I did, all kinds of walls came down, including a few that revealed similar preconceptions held by churches all over the world. As things began to fall into place, I felt a sense of freedom that my own mind had kept from me. Looking back, had my breakthrough occurred during that class, I might have failed the exam.

While this chronological mindset is imposed *upon* the text, I did discover a related issue that exists *within* the text. As you study, you may detect how John's choice of words can lead us to believe that he experienced a linear sequence of events. His use of the phrase "and then," specifically, mimics the way you and I describe what happens *next* in a series. Yet John used this phrase to introduce something new. And that new thing is often what triggers an event he already told us about. This occurs on multiple occasions. And we'll only catch it when we understand the *overall* order of things as presented throughout the Bible. For those of you who've been tripped up by this, you can argue semantics with John when you see him in heaven. I'll let you borrow my grammar hammer if you promise to give it back.

666

As fascinated as I am by numbers, I won't even begin to count the misconceptions surrounding the number 666. So, I'll just address some of the more prominent ones, beginning with the idea that this number represents some kind of bad omen. I remember my mom throwing out a check in her checkbook because its number had 666 in it. I also read about some guy who swore that he would never read page 666 in any book. And I was like, how many books with this number of pages is this dude reading??? So, for the nervous Nellies out there, you can rest assured that, until this number is stamped on your forehead by a member of the Antichrist's army, it's merely the number that comes after 665. But you have my blessing if you choose to rage against being issued a satanic license plate. It would be okay to do it then, I think.

Next, we can talk about how people will be marked with this number. Aside from *where* this number will be placed on one's body, the Bible tells us nothing about the method used to put it there. And yet theories abound, supposing everything from barcode tattoos to microchip injections. My thoughts on this? As much as I love movies, I do recognize that there's a point when a person has watched too many. The receipt of the beast's mark could involve a branding iron or a Sharpie for all we know. The fact that this debate exists at all is weird enough. So, I'm staying out of it.

Lastly, I'll point out how God has given us a challenge concerning 666 that involves doing a bit of math. Despite being a total nerd when it comes to numbers in the Bible, I know better than to spend any time on this. But I have indeed seen a multitude of attempts at this challenge by people who... got stuck in traffic on the way to the movie theater. People have actually been at this for ages. So, let's dive in and see what this is all about.

Here is wisdom. Let him who has understanding calculate the number of the beast, for the number is that of a man; and his number is six hundred and sixty-six.

Revelation 13:18

Here we see that 666 is somehow tied to the Antichrist's name or identity. Due to the popular understanding that this number is all we have to go on, many have come up with all kinds of crazy ways to pin it on public figures and label them as objects of God's wrath. Had they watched the entire movie, they'd know that God has already identified this man for us. We have all the info we need to recognize the Antichrist when we see him. And we'll look at some of this information shortly. Our challenge is the *calculation*, or figuring out *how* this number is attached to his identity. Here's how we do it.

In the equation **2+x=4**, '2' is a constant (the Antichrist), 'x' is a variable, and '4' is the answer (666). And our task is to solve for x. Those who are oblivious to the Antichrist's identity, however, are trying to solve for the constant *and* the variable. While the Bible tells us plenty about this man, we have to know his name before we can even begin this challenge. Otherwise, we'd be infringing upon an important ground rule God gave us—a rule that countless authors, teachers, influencers, and prophecy-centered ministries have apparently never read.

But know this first of all, that no prophecy of Scripture is a matter of one's own interpretation.

2 Peter 1:20

Boom! This is the Bible's mic drop if there ever was one. It assures us that everyone trying to identify the Antichrist using 666 not only missed the first part of the movie, but they left the theater before the movie even ended! The beauty of this little challenge is that we can't screw it up. We may not be able to solve it when the time comes, but the constant and the answer are fixed. Therefore, the solution can add nothing to the Bible. God has not given us an instruction to "finish" His Word by becoming prophecy detectives. All mysteries have either been solved already or will be solved through God's revelations—not ours. I'd drop my own mic here, but I need it for the audiobook.

THE HORROR

In the book of Malachi, the day of Christ's return is described as both great and terrible. And yet many of us tend to regard the 'great' as a measure of the terrible. I've done this too, so I'm not pointing any fingers. Despite having the complete assurance of my salvation, the picture Jesus paints in Matthew is scary as hell.

Not everyone who says to Me, 'Lord, Lord,' will enter the kingdom of heaven, but he who does the will of My Father who is in heaven will enter. Many will say to Me on that day, 'Lord, Lord, did we not prophesy in Your name, and in Your name cast out demons, and in Your name perform many miracles?' And then I will declare

to them, 'I never knew you; depart from Me, you who practice lawlessness.'

Matthew 7:21-23

When it comes to the fears we have about the events described in Revelation, our tendency to let them override feelings of joy and victory cannot be blamed on the Bible. Rather, this anxiety appears to be fueled by worldly influences. The fact that our churches are becoming increasingly hesitant to teach Revelation may play into this fear as well, driving those interested in the topic toward "Christian" conspiracy theorists who are happy to do the talking. Even if this was not the case, the church isn't exactly off the hook concerning this ominous view of the end times. In addition to labeling the seven years with *tribulation* instead of *restoration*, we traded one of the most beautiful words in the Bible with one that belongs in the title of a horror movie. Thus, our day of *redemption* became the *rapture*. Yeah, we're weird. I just hope we don't end up calling saints in heaven *transformers*. You know, because we will all be "transformed." Yeah, you get it.

The infusion of technology and AI into Scripture also has many of us on edge. While concerns over how AI is being used in our world today are certainly valid, none of us should anticipate digital domination leaving our world with no church left to rapture. The same can be said of environmental issues, such as global warming choking out the population or scorching the whole of humanity. I'm all for any effort to make the world a better and safer place to live, but the end is written. We all know what's coming. And yet, far too many of us live in fear over scenarios that we've allowed others to put into our heads. I get it, though. This world does indeed seem to be spiraling in a dark direction. And Jesus did tell us that the generations to come would be evil and adulterous. But you and I aren't going down with this ship. We're getting the heck out of Dodge, vacating the premises, and hitting the road, Jack! As for when this permanent vacation will begin, there's an awful lot of speculation among those who missed the first part of the movie. So, let's finish this thing together once and for all.

RAPTURE

Believe it or not, the one book believed to have all the available info about the end times never mentions the rapture—not even once. Because of this, the understanding that the entirety of Revelation occurs after the rapture is quite common. Even if we were given a clear reference to the rapture, we still couldn't use Revelation to determine when it will occur without first having an overarching timeline with fixed boundaries to plug all these events and blocks of time into. Thankfully, that timeline is provided for us. It's just not in Revelation.

Now, I did say that I wasn't going to dive into all the end-times events that are presented outside of Revelation. And I'm not—not *all* of them anyway. This rapture lesson wasn't even included in my original outline. But I'm here to explain all of this. And we're going to encounter verses that will lead us straight down that rabbit hole.

I'm not complaining, though. I absolutely love teaching this topic, so I'm pleased that this book gives me yet another opportunity to do so. Before we move on, let me point out that this area of study can make your head spin a little, so prepare to focus. Or, as Samuel L. Jackson would say, hold on to your butts!

Before God showed me how to put these pieces together, I had almost given into the idea that we simply cannot know when the rapture will occur. Regardless of where I sought help, there was always someone who pointed out how Jesus said we can't know "the day or the hour" (Matt. 24:36, Mark 13:32). Eventually, I did what I should have done at the very beginning—examine the question Jesus was replying to. So, were the disciples asking about the rapture? No. Given their responses when Jesus told them about it, I'm not sure they had a firm grasp on the topic yet. But Mary's sister Martha sure did! Her brief dissertation on eschatology gets an A+ in my book (John 11:24). Anyway, instead of inquiring about when they would be leaving, the disciples wanted to know when Jesus was coming back. And these two events do not happen on the same day.

But of that day or hour no one knows, not even the angels in heaven, nor the Son, but the Father alone.

Mark 13:32

As followers of Christ, you and I will indeed know the day and the hour. How is that possible? It's because we'll be *with* Jesus when he returns. We may not know until the moment it happens, but we won't be caught off guard the way people on the earth stand to be. This will become clear in the chapters ahead if it isn't already. Anyway, contrary to the idea that we as God's church are waiting *here* for Jesus to return, the earth is definitely not where we'll be when he does.

THE CONUNDRUM

While the events that make up the rapture are rarely in dispute, we tend to take sides over *when* we believe it will occur. These positions are tied to where we believe this day falls within the tribulation period. One who believes that the rapture will occur *before* these seven years may refer to its occurrence as *pre-tribulation*. And then there are those who hold a *mid-tribulation* view that places the rapture in the *middle* of this period. To complicate matters even further, there's confusion over whether these stances relate to the actual tribulation or the tribulation *period*. While there is indeed a view of the rapture as occurring *post-tribulation*, this perspective essentially undermines the central message of the Christian faith. So, with all these options to haggle over, one might choose to just throw up their hands and side with those who say we can't know. But they'd be missing the fact that we can.

DISTRESS SIGNAL

Now, in order to pinpoint the timing of the Rapture, we must create a biblical cocktail of sorts, combining Scripture from both the Old and New Testaments. As for our guides in this endeavor, Jesus and Daniel will take the lead and point us all in the right direction. And we'll begin with Jesus' words from that same conversation with his disciples that we just looked at.

Therefore, when you see the abomination of desolation which was spoken of through Daniel the prophet, standing in the holy place—let the reader understand—then those who are in Judea must flee to the mountains.

For those days will be such a time of tribulation as has not occurred since the beginning of the creation which God created until now, and never will again.

Mark 13:14, 19

Here, Jesus gives the instruction to evacuate when the Antichrist shows up to take over the temple. This will cause Jerusalem to become desolate—hence, the abomination of *desolation*. He also spoke of some unprecedented distress that will begin around the time this happens. While there are multiple books in the Bible that teach us this, Jesus pointed us to Daniel's. So, let's go there and see what he had to say about this.

And there will be a time of distress such as never occurred since there was a nation until that time; and at that time your people, everyone who is found written in the book, will be rescued.

Daniel 12:1

In this text that Jesus was quoting, we see that Daniel took this information a step further, including the rapture as also being tied to the beginning of this great distress. And the rapture, of course, is our rescue from the tribulation that the appearance of the abomination sets in motion. So, the abomination, the rapture, and the distress all occur around the same time. You with me so far? Good. Now, all that's left to do is find out when this abomination is going to show up.

From the time that the regular sacrifice is abolished and the abomination of desolation is set up, there will be 1,290 days.

Daniel 12:11

Returning to the explanation of the 70 weeks that Daniel was given, here are the details of the final week, or seven years.

And he will make a firm covenant with the many for one week, but in the middle of the week he will put a stop to sacrifice and grain offering; and on the wing

of abominations will come one who makes desolate, even until a complete destruction, one that is decreed, is poured out on the one who makes desolate.

Daniel 9:27

In addition to rebuilding the temple, Israel intends to reinstate the sacrificial worship that God commanded them to carry out in Leviticus. And we know this will eventually come to fruition because the Antichrist will put a stop to it right smack in the middle of the seven years. Also, since half of seven years is only 1,260 days according to Scripture (a year is 360 days), we're told there will be an additional 30 days after the seven-year period concludes. So, in response to Daniel's question about when life on earth would come to a complete end, we are informed that the entire end-times saga will last seven years and one month (2,550 days)—peace on the first day, the earth's destruction on the last. This is that overarching timeline we've been needing. Now, back to the rapture.

Between the abomination, the distress, and the rapture, only the abomination event is said to occur on a specific day (1,261). The other two are described as happening "at that time." Given the vast timeline we're working with, a reasonable proximity might be days, weeks, or even within a few months. So, if we rest here, we can say that the rapture will happen shortly after the midpoint of the seven years, thus ending the whole pre-trib/mid-trib debacle. But we're not resting here because the Bible isn't done. Indeed, there's one more piece of information to examine.

BLESSING IN DISGUISE

Keep in mind that the information that we're using to build this timeline comes from an angel in response to Daniel's questions about the timing of the end. Much like the disciples, he wanted to know the *when* of things. While Jesus could not provide the specifics, this angel spilled his guts. Ooh, that sentence didn't end well. Let's say he... sang like a canary! He spilled the beans?? There's an idiom that works here. Maybe one that doesn't sound like the angel is confessing to a crime. I'll look for a better one. Anyway, the angel didn't reveal what Jesus kept closed-lipped about. They were talking about separate events. But you knew that.

From the time that the regular sacrifice is abolished and the abomination of desolation is set up, there will be 1,290 days. How blessed is he who keeps waiting and attains to the 1,335 days!

Daniel 12:11-12

Here, you'll see a verse that we've already looked at together. This time, I included the very next one that tells us how those who are blessed will be patient and "hang in there" until day 1,335. There's also an exclamation point! Now, the Bible doesn't actually say that this day is the rapture. But there are some things worth considering. First, if we examine the question Daniel asked of the angel, we see that this day is a significant one within the timeline. Because 1,290 days get us from the midpoint of the seven years to the very last day, 1,335 must be counted from day one. Next, we see that day 1,335 is less than three months away from the abomination, making it easy to describe as being *around* that time. Finally, one's "blessed" status is not contingent upon reaching this day. There's no *if* involved. Rather, reaching day 1,335 is what those who *are* blessed will do. When used as an adjective in the Bible, the word *blessed* describes those who are *saved*. You can swap between these two words in every verse that includes "blessed is he," "blessed are they," etc., and the context remains intact. So, if the rapture occurs any earlier than the 1,335th day, there will be no blessed people to attain to it. Feel free to read this paragraph again if you need to. It's kind of a doozie.

MY CONCLUSION

So, Daniel tells us what Revelation doesn't, and Revelation tells us what Daniel doesn't. And still more books must be considered before we can see the entire picture. This analysis is even abbreviated compared to the one in my other book, which you can check out if you're a nerd for this stuff like I am. So, do I believe that the rapture will happen 1,335 days into the seven years? The Bible certainly makes a good case for it. And we may actually be able to wait and see about this one. The rapture's occurrence in the middle of the seven years is pretty ironclad, though. And that's all we need in order to better understand Revelation.

Now, about that idiom I didn't quite nail earlier. Here are some alternatives I found. Unfortunately, I'm not completely sold on any of these. So, I'll leave it up to you to insert the one you like the best.

The angel...

...let the cat out of the bag.
...gave Daniel the 411.
...spilled the beans.
...kept Daniel in the loop.

I'll let you know if I find any more.

THE CAST

Every movie has a cast of characters. The actors who portray those characters are chosen based on how well a director believes they will embody their roles. The ultimate goal, of course, comes down to one question. Will people buy it? Similarly, the Bible is filled with characters that God has chosen to achieve His will on earth. Unlike movie directors who can only hope that everyone will buy a ticket, God's design for this world includes those who won't. In Revelation, God gives us a glimpse of how life will play out among those who wait until after the rapture to surrender to Jesus. We refer to this group as the *tribulation saints*. And John saw how they will be given white robes upon their arrival in heaven after being killed during the great distress that raptured saints will be spared. As for those who will die during this period without having trusted in Jesus, the Bible refers to them as "the others." Only members of these two groups may witness the entire cast of characters that we'll get acquainted with now.

THE ANTICHRIST (aka King of the South)

Among the numerous books of the Bible that speak of this figure, it is Daniel's that gives us a proper introduction. In his seventh chapter, the scene is similar to that of Revelation, where an angel explained the visuals Daniel was seeing. The visual in question involves a little horn (a prince) rising up among ten bigger horns (kings). And when this prince shows up, three of the kings disappear. That leaves us with seven big horns along with the little one, whose actions become a focal point of Daniel's vision. This is the Antichrist.

I kept looking, and that horn was waging war with the saints and overpowering them until the Ancient of Days came and judgment was passed in favor of the saints of the Highest One...
Daniel 7:21-22

In my research, I found 27 chapters within the Bible that speak of the Antichrist. Some passages merely give him a mention while others outline his character, behavior, whereabouts, etc. Instead of providing us with a name, the Bible describes this ominous figure as both a *man* and a *beast*. While Daniel focuses on the man, his role as a beast is fleshed out in Revelation, along with an event that may serve as the point of transition between these two forms.

> **Then the king of the South will grow strong, along with one of his princes who will gain ascendancy over him and obtain dominion; his domain will be a great dominion indeed.**
>
> **Daniel 11:5**

As we read on, we learn that the Antichrist will be the crown prince of a very wealthy nation located to the south of Israel, and that he may assume the responsibilities of king before actually taking the throne. While his crowning is not mentioned, Revelation assures us that he will be king when he brokers the big peace agreement on the very first day of the seven years. In this next verse that we'll look at again later, we're informed that he will be the eighth king to rule over his nation and that he will be a member of a group of seven kings. This lines up with Daniel's vision of the 8 horns (7 kings and 1 prince). When the prince takes his father's throne, we'll be left with 7 kings.

> **The beast who once was, and now is not, is an eighth king. He belongs to the seven and is going to his destruction.**
>
> **Revelation 17:11**

The members of this group are believed to be the nations that will sign on to the Antichrist's peace accord. This seems fitting as it would require at least this many nations to put an end to the chaos in the Middle East. If this is the case, the Antichrist's own nation will be among those who sign on. Next, we're informed of the Antichrist's role as a reformer whose actions represent a departure from the way his father and previous kings had run things.

He shall enter peaceably even into the richest places of the province; and he shall do that which his fathers have not done, nor his fathers' fathers.

...he will intend to change the times and the law

Daniel 11:24, 7:25

While there's more we can know about this man, this will suffice until we become acquainted with his role as a beast. Already, there's enough information here to assure us that no two men can match his description. Just as the Highlander would say, "There can be only one." Soon, we'll look at how the Antichrist will earn his title of "great deceiver" as both a man and a beast.

KING OF THE NORTH

This title is given to a nation located to the north of Israel. Paired with the names "Gog" and "Magog" in Ezekiel, the latter being the son of Japheth (Noah's son), this is the home of the Scythian people, who were the first to settle in the land we now call Russia. And Daniel's angel informed us of this nation's behavior at the time of the end, which is consistent with what we're seeing of Russia today.

He will invade many countries and sweep through them like a flood.

Daniel 11:40

In Revelation, we read how God will move this king to gather the armies of its allies and attack Israel. While Ezekiel provides the most details of this attack, we can read about it all the way back in the book Numbers.

And you will say, 'I will go up against the land of unwalled villages. I will go against those who are at rest, that live securely, all of them living without walls and having no bars or gates, to capture spoil and to seize plunder...

You will advance against my people Israel like a cloud that covers the land.

Ezekiel 38:11-12, 16

To provide some context, the Old Testament books inform us that the Northern armies will take advantage of the peace agreement initiated by the Antichrist. Desiring "a great spoil," which I suspect includes Israel's oil, this merger of armed forces will target the Holy Land while its defenses are down. When the southern king (Antichrist) gets wind of this, he and his army will rush in to occupy and subdue Israel.

And it appears that the Antichrist will seize the temple and use it as his headquarters as he waits for the northern armies to show up. This is the abomination event that Jesus and Daniel spoke of. And because we're given the very days associated with these moves, it is highly likely that members of God's church will be around to watch all of this on the news. Finally, we're told that the kings of the north and south will have a relationship and appear to be aligned with one another—an alliance that will surely end when the Antichrist realizes that he is about to be betrayed.

The two kings, with their hearts bent on evil, will sit at the same table and lie to each other, but to no avail, because an end will still come at the appointed time.

Daniel 11:47

TWO WITNESSES

Two! Two witnesses! Ah ah ah! I guess there are only so many numbers one can toss around without bringing up The Count from Sesame Street. These are the two hooded fellows on the cover of this book, by the way. Despite being very prominent figures in Revelation, I'd never seen anyone capture them in artwork before. So, I took a risk knowing that some of you may not have put two and two together until now. There's a pun in that last sentence. I'm sure of it.

Unlike the Antichrist, who will have an ID card and a physical address, these two men could serve as black ops agents, as their identities will be completely untraceable. Their mission, however, will be anything but covert. According to Scripture, these two men will have lived out their lives on earth back when a census involved traveling on foot and disobedient prophets were swallowed by whales. So, they'll have been in God's presence for a very long time before they are sent back to earth. While their identities are obscured, Malachi leaked one of their names. Spoiler alert!

Behold, I am going to send you Elijah the prophet before the coming of the great and terrible day of the Lord.

Malachi 4:5

Revelation actually gives us clues to both their identities. And we'll examine those clues in the chapters ahead. As we learned previously, these two witnesses will be here during the first half of the seven years to prepare 144,000 more witnesses who'll serve as lights in the darkness amidst the tribulation of the second half. And it's in the middle of this period that these two men will experience death for the second time when the Antichrist kills them on his way to take over the temple. This, too, is an event that appears to occur before the rapture.

THE FALSE PROPHET

Much like Satan or demons, this false prophet is sometimes regarded as having an otherworldly nature. This is due to Scripture's lack of character development that ties him to the earth. There's definitely an air of mystery surrounding the Antichrist's right-hand man, which I believe sums up his role quite well. Despite the lack of revealing details, however, we are assured that this prominent figure in Revelation is indeed a human man. God has simply chosen to reveal more about his connections than the man himself. And there are two full chapters dedicated to informing us about the entity with which he's affiliated—a worldwide church that the Bible calls "the great whore."

In my walkthrough of Revelation that I'll kick off after this chapter, I will mirror the Bible's effort to expose this church that we are informed is active in our world today. This narrative encompasses chapters 17 and 18 and can be a bit confusing if you're not given a proper introduction. When I first started teaching, I decided to skip these two chapters when presenting a similar walkthrough of Revelation to a small group at church, and not because I was afraid they wouldn't understand them. It was because I didn't. I also didn't want to read the word "whore" aloud in church, so there's that. But I became determined not to skip over them again.

Today, I regard these chapters as the most important of the 22, as they represent an urgent call to action for people all over the world who've been led astray by this church's false teaching. We who embrace the true gospel also have a responsibility to recognize this institution and share God's truth with our friends and loved ones whose hearts are ensnared by its influence. The Bible does not call out this church by name, but those who are blessed will certainly know it and "take to heart" what is written according to the Bible's declaration at the beginning and ending of this book. While God's contempt for the false prophet is evident in Revelation, the degree to which God detests this man's church appears to be at its peak.

JESUS CHRIST

The earth was formed by the one true God—a heavenly and perfect being who is not of the world. He made the world to accommodate humanity, which He also created out of love. When God saw that humans were sinful and imperfect beings, He sent His son to live among us, to teach us, and to bear witness to God, our heavenly Father. His name was, and still is, Jesus.

Jesus, who is God incarnate, was born to a virgin in the city of Bethlehem and lived as a human man free of all imperfection. At around age 30, Jesus left his home in Nazareth in search of twelve men whom he would befriend and teach the manner in which we are to love one another, and who would share his words with the world after Jesus' objective to serve as a living sacrifice was complete.

Jesus' sacrifice was his own suffering and death by crucifixion. This act served as a means by which the sins of all humans may be forgiven. By taking on the punishment we deserve, Jesus' death made it possible for humans to be redeemed through salvation. To validate his divinity as the son of the living God, Jesus arose from the tomb in which his body lay for three days.

After his resurrection, and after visiting with his disciples and being seen by more than 500 people, Jesus ascended into heaven, where he sits at God's right hand even today. Those who knew and learned from Jesus were moved by God's Spirit to write down the things he did and all that he taught them. These testimonies are recorded in the Holy Bible. And in the Bible, we are assured that all who believe and place their trust in Jesus, the Savior of the world, will not perish but be rewarded with eternal life on a new earth in God's presence and in fellowship with Jesus and with one another forever.

REVELATION 1 & 2
Jesus surprises John with a writing assignment.

CHAPTER 1

Revelation begins with a declaration that this book contains a vision of future events which God gave Jesus to share with us. The details were delivered to the Apostle John, the youngest of the twelve disciples, who served as a first-hand witness to Jesus and to all the things that Jesus did and said. Here, God applies the word "blessed" to all who will read, understand, and obey the words that are written in this book.

Blessed is he who reads and those who hear the words of the prophecy, and heed the things which are written in it; for the time is near.

1:3

Next, we read a preamble for messages that John is preparing to write, which will be delivered in the form of letters to seven prominent churches in Asia Minor.

Grace to you and peace, from Him who is and who was and who is to come, and from the seven Spirits who are before His throne, and from Jesus Christ, the faithful witness, the firstborn of the dead, and the ruler of the kings of the earth.

1:4-5

John then added that he was writing from the island of Patmos, where he was placed for sharing his testimony of Jesus. Upon hearing a voice behind him instructing him to write down all that he was about to witness, John turned and saw the risen and glorified Jesus, whose appearance he described in detail. John then fainted and fell to the ground at Jesus' feet.

Then I turned to see the voice that was speaking with me. And after turning I saw seven golden lampstands; and in the middle of the lampstands I saw one like a son of man, clothed in a robe reaching to the feet, and wrapped around the chest with a golden sash. His head and His hair were white like white wool, like snow; and His eyes were like a flame of fire. His feet were like burnished bronze when it has been heated to a glow in a furnace, and His voice was like the sound of many waters. In His right hand He held seven stars, and out of His mouth came a sharp two-edged sword; and His face was like the sun shining in its strength.

1:12-16

Jesus then comforted John with the assurance that it was his friend and Savior who was visiting him that day, and went on to explain the purpose of his visit. John understood that he was to create a written record of the things he had seen in the past and present, as well as the presentation he was about to see, which would inform him of things to come.

Write, therefore, what you have seen, what is now and what will take place later.

1:19

This record also included messages that Jesus would dictate and that John would include in his letters to the seven churches, which were located in the cities of Ephesus, Smyrna, Pergamum, Thyatira, Sardis, Philadelphia, and Laodicea. As for the pastors of these churches, they are believed to be made up of John's and the Apostle Paul's own disciples. At the close of this chapter, Jesus explained that the stars John saw him holding represented these seven pastors, and that the lampstands that also appeared with him stood for the churches themselves.

Due to John sharing his preamble for these letters up front, it would seem that Jesus interrupted his writing. Because Jesus' instruction included writing these letters, and because John obviously was not expecting him, we may conclude that Jesus appeared *before* John began to write. As you will see, this is the first of many events he presented out of order.

CHAPTER 2

In this second chapter, we read the contents of the first four letters to the churches as they were spoken aloud by Jesus. Here, we learn that each letter served as a report card of sorts, offering passing and failing grades according to the practices and attitudes that each church fostered. And each of Jesus' messages conveyed his awareness of what was going on.

To the angel of the church in Ephesus write: The One who holds the seven stars in His right hand, the One who walks among the seven golden lampstands, says this: I know your deeds and your labor and perseverance, and that you cannot tolerate evil people, and you have put those who call themselves apostles to the test, and they are not, and you found them to be false; and you have perseverance and have endured on account of My name, and have not become weary. But I have this against you, that you have left your first love.

2:1-4

After pointing out how the church's love for him had gone cold, Jesus concluded his message to Ephesus with an instruction for the congregation to repent and to return to the manner in which they worshiped when the church first began. While Jesus did commend the church members' mutual hatred for the practices of the Nicolaitans, a group not mentioned elsewhere in the Bible, this wasn't enough for them to escape his warning against continuing in their ways.

Repent and do the things you did at first. If you do not repent, I will come to you and remove your lampstand from its place.

2:5

In the remaining three messages that conclude this chapter, the church at Smyrna was encouraged to remain steadfast during a ten-day period when they would be tested by Satan. This was necessary to purge the congregation of those who falsely claimed to be Jews. Whether these were gentiles posing as Jews for one reason or another, or simply not what Jesus would call true Israelites (John 1:47) is not made clear. But it was a serious issue that Jesus will point out again in these letters.

Do not be afraid of what you are about to suffer. I tell you, the devil will put some of you in prison to test you, and you will suffer persecution for ten days. Be faithful, even to the point of death, and I will give you life as your victor's crown.

2:10

After commending the strides taken at Pergamum to remain on the right path, Jesus shared his concern over how the church had allowed false teaching to penetrate its doctrine. And to Thyatira, the son of man expressed his condemnation of their allowing the self-proclaimed prophetess, Jezebel, to influence its church members to eat food that had been sacrificed to idols and to engage in sexual immorality. Jesus also recognized that not everyone had fallen into her clutches.

Now I say to the rest of you in Thyatira, to you who do not hold to her teaching and have not learned Satan's so-called deep secrets, 'I will not impose any other burden on you, except to hold on to what you have until I come.'

2:24-25

REVELATION 3 & 4

John's sees heaven after completing the last three letters.

CHAPTER 3

In his fifth letter, addressed to the church at Sardis, Jesus issued a familiar warning that is echoed in the books of 1 Thessalonians and 2 Peter. Save for a few members who were walking uprightly, the church was charged with being spiritually dead. As a result, those who remained complacent stood to regard Christ's return in the same manner one reacts to being robbed unexpectedly by a thief.

Be constantly alert, and strengthen the things that remain, which are about to die; for I have not found your deeds completed in the sight of My God. So remember what you have received and heard; and keep it, and repent. Then if you are not alert, I will come like a thief, and you will not know at what hour I will come to you.

3:2-3

In his sixth letter, which is free of condemnations, Jesus praised the church at Philadelphia for its congregation's perseverance and swift dealings with those who falsely claimed to be Jews, thus negating their need to be tested the way Smyrna did. Jesus concluded this letter by urging the church to press on.

Because you have kept My word of perseverance, I also will keep you from the hour of the testing, that hour which is about to come upon the whole world, to test those who live on the earth. I am coming quickly; hold firmly to what you have, so that no one will take your crown.

3:10-11

In his seventh and final letter, Jesus addressed how wealth had impacted the church members at Laodicea in his renowned "lukewarm" speech. If you've ever wondered how Jesus could regard both hot and cold temperatures as pleasing, know that his allegory was not a measure of one's attitude toward him. While the benefits of hot and cold against aches and pains are widely speculated to be what Jesus was referring to, I like to teach this in terms of how you and I like our coffee... and how we don't.

So, because you are lukewarm—neither hot nor cold—I am about to spit you out of my mouth.

3:16

Just as the woman at the well was informed of the life-giving water she could obtain from Jesus, congregants at Laodicea were urged to buy his gold, which was "refined by fire" in order to rise above the spiritual blindness that plagued the church. In this next verse, Jesus used the equivalent of our "Hellooo??" to convey feeling invisible to a congregation that was fixated on anything but him.

Here I am! I stand at the door and knock. If anyone hears my voice and opens the door, I will come in and eat with that person, and they with me.

3:20

CHAPTER 4

After completing the seven letters, John was given a vision of a doorway that Jesus' voice beckoned him to enter. Here, John describes himself as being "in the Spirit" as he is brought before the awe-inducing splendor of God's throne. This is the first scene he encountered without having utilized his physical body's five senses.

Immediately I was in the Spirit; and behold, a throne was standing in heaven, and someone was sitting on the throne. And He who was sitting was like a jasper stone and a sardius in appearance; and there was a rainbow around the throne, like an emerald in

appearance. Around the throne were twenty-four thrones; and upon the thrones I saw twenty-four elders sitting, clothed in white garments, and golden crowns on their heads.

4:2-4

John goes on to describe lightning and peals of thunder that radiated from the throne, as well as four living creatures having the appearances of a lion, a calf, a flying eagle, and another having a human face. Each having six wings and an array of eyes covering their front and back, these four creatures continually offered praises to God.

And the four living creatures, each one of them having six wings, are full of eyes around and within; and day and night they do not cease to say, "Holy, holy, holy is the Lord God, the Almighty, who was and who is and who is to come."

4:8

With each of these praises, a group of 24 elders followed suit by falling down before the throne and offering praises of their own.

Worthy are You, our Lord and our God, to receive glory and honor and power; for You created all things, and because of Your will they existed, and were created.

4:11

Given that the title *elder* was commonly attributed to humans in John's day, we may conclude that the 24 he described as elders were depictions of human men. As I mentioned earlier, many believe that 12 of these elders were Jesus' disciples. If this were the case, then John himself would be among them. As for those who've taken this into account, some suppose that the reason John did not recognize himself or his friends was either that he was not close enough to see their faces, or that the disciples were all depicted as old men (elders) and not immediately recognizable. As for me, I err on the side of this all being a vision.

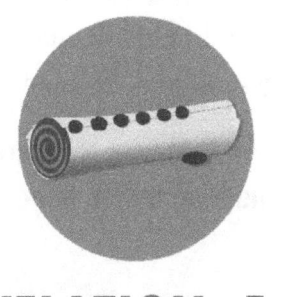

REVELATION 5 & 6

God is praised and a scroll is opened.

CHAPTER 5

Amidst the wonders that John was seeing all around him, his attention was drawn to a scroll that God held in His right hand. As he examined the appearance of the scroll, he saw that it was held closed by seven seals. It was then that a mighty angel asked in a loud voice who among those present was worthy to open the scroll and view what was written on it. When no one immediately stepped forward, John's emotions got the best of him.

Then I began to weep greatly because no one was found worthy to open the scroll or to look into it. And one of the elders said to me, "Stop weeping; behold, the Lion that is from the tribe of Judah, the Root of David, has overcome so as to be able to open the scroll and its seven seals."

5:4-5

When Jesus came forward, the creatures and elders all fell down to worship him while thousands upon thousands of angels offered their praises to the Lamb.

Worthy is the Lamb that was slaughtered to receive power, wealth, wisdom, might, honor, glory, and blessing.

5:12

The praises by multitudes of angels were followed by more praises that came from every created being, whether human or animal, in heaven and on the earth. You may have sung this stanza yourself in church. I know I have.

To Him who sits on the throne and to the Lamb be the blessing, the honor, the glory, and the dominion forever and ever.

5:13

CHAPTER 6

John continues his written record of things to come by describing the first of multiple series of moving images that were presented to him inside the throne room. While the number of images within each group varied, each set was crafted to inform John how the world will progress toward the end in increasing detail. As Jesus broke the first of the scroll's seven seals, one of the creatures with six wings and eyes all over called forth a rider on a white horse whose purpose was to achieve victory. This image is often associated with the peace that the Antichrist will bring on the first day of the tribulation period.

Then I saw when the Lamb broke one of the seven seals, and I heard one of the four living creatures saying as with a voice of thunder, "Come!" I looked, and behold, a white horse, and the one who sat on it had a bow; and a crown was given to him, and he went out conquering and to conquer.

6:1-2

When the second seal was removed, another of the creatures beckoned the image of a rider on a red horse who was given the instruction to end peace by inciting a war on the earth.

And another, a red horse, went out; and to him who sat on it, it was granted to take peace from the earth, and that people would kill one another; and a large sword was given to him.

6:4

When Jesus removed the scroll's third seal, a rider on a black horse was summoned. This image was to inform John of a famine that war on the earth would bring about. And the breaking of the fourth seal prompted a creature to call forth a gray horse. Its rider, whose name was Death, was followed by another figure named Hades. These two were given authority over a quarter of the earth to kill with war, famine, plague, and by wild animals. Together, these images are commonly referred to as the 'Four Horsemen of the Apocalypse,' especially in movies about the end of the world.

Instead of another rider on a horse, the breaking of the fifth seal revealed an image of those who had arrived in heaven after being killed on the earth for their testimony of Jesus. Desiring vengeance, they cried out to God and asked when He would deal with those who had killed them.

Then each of them was given a white robe, and they were told to wait a little longer, until the full number of their fellow servants, their brothers and sisters, were killed just as they had been.

6:11

When Jesus broke the sixth seal, John was shown a great earthquake that caused every mountain on earth to fall and every island to be swallowed up by the sea. This scene included a darkened sun and a blood-red moon. As the stars fell from the heavens, John watched as the sky disappeared as if being rolled up like a scroll. The cries of the people who took cover inside caverns suggest that heaven will be visible to those on earth when this event occurs in the future.

They called to the mountains and the rocks, "Fall on us and hide us from the face of him who sits on the throne and from the wrath of the Lamb! For the great day of their wrath has come, and who can withstand it?"

6:16

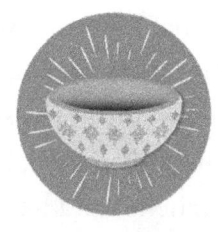

REVELATION 7 & 8

Martyrs are given robes. Angels are given trumpets.

CHAPTER 7

As the imagery sparked by the breaking of the sixth seal continued, John saw four angels stationed at the four corners of the earth. These were instructed by yet another angel not to allow devastation to the land and the sea until all 144,000 of God's servants were "sealed" with a mark on their foreheads that would make them unharmed by what was coming. Comprised of 12,000 people from each of Israel's twelve family lines, this group's members will take up positions all over the world and share the gospel publicly after the rapture.

Then I saw another angel ascending from the rising of the sun, with the seal of the living God, and he called with a loud voice to the four angels who had been given power to harm earth and sea, saying, "Do not harm the earth or the sea or the trees, until we have sealed the servants of our God on their foreheads."

7:2-3

After this, the scene that John was watching shifted back to those in white robes who had been killed on the earth for their testimony of Jesus. Not only had this group grown tremendously in size, but its members now carried palm branches and had traded their vengeful pleas for shouts of praise.

And they cried out in a loud voice: "Salvation belongs to our God, who sits on the throne, and to the Lamb."
7:10

As the four creatures and 24 elders joined the worship that was occurring in this scene, an angel inside the throne room spoke to John and asked him if he understood who these people were, each having been killed and wearing white robes. After pointing out that it was the angel who had that info, John was told that they came from every nation during a time of great tribulation and that their robes had been made clean by the blood of the lamb. The angel then explained how God will shelter and provide for them on the new earth.

They will hunger no longer, nor thirst anymore; nor will the sun beat down on them, nor any heat; for the Lamb in the center of the throne will be their shepherd, and will guide them to springs of the water of life; and God will wipe every tear from their eyes.
7:16-17

CHAPTER 8

When the Lamb broke the seventh seal, there was silence in heaven for about half an hour.

8:1

In this portion of John's vision, we begin to see overlapping groups of events. In the same way that a photographer sees new details with each level of a camera's zoom, each group provides increasingly detailed information. Without any zoom applied, the four horsemen provided a high-level overview of the timeline in four stages—peace, war, famine, and death. After this, we zoomed in on the lives of the people who will experience the distress of an earthquake, a darkened sun, and other destructive plagues that will occur during these 4 stages. And we're about to zoom in even closer to learn about events that are the direct result of these plagues. As for the triggers that ushered in these new images for John, the sound of trumpets picked up where the breaking of the seals left off.

As we read on, we learn how John's attention was directed toward a group of angels. Seven were given trumpets as one angel approached an altar with a golden bowl filled with the prayers of the saints. After adding incense to the bowl and lighting it with fire from the altar, the angel added its embers to a censer and then tossed the censer down onto the earth.

This resulted in lightning, thunder, and a great earthquake. This also prompted the seven other angels to begin blowing their trumpets one at a time.

The first angel blew his trumpet, and there followed hail and fire, mixed with blood, and these were thrown upon the earth. And a third of the earth was burned up, and a third of the trees were burned up, and all green grass was burned up.

8:7

When the second angel blew his trumpet, John saw an image of a giant flaming star among those falling to the earth. As big as a mountain in size, this star landed in the sea, causing a third of the water to become blood. As John watched, a third of the sea's ships were destroyed along with a third of its sea life. At the sound of the third angel's trumpet, another giant star poisoned a third of the fresh water sources (rivers, streams), which killed many who drank from them. This star was given the name 'Wormwood.'

The fourth angel's trumpet also impacted a third of its targets—the sun and the moon, whose light was hidden during a third of the earth's daytime and nighttime hours. As the chapter comes to a close, John tells us about a frightening announcement made by an eagle he saw soaring in the skies above the earth.

As I watched, I heard an eagle that was flying in midair call out in a loud voice: "Woe! Woe! Woe to the inhabitants of the earth, because of the trumpet blasts about to be sounded by the other three angels!"

8:13

REVELATION 9 & 10

The earth is plagued, and John eats a book.

CHAPTER 9

At the sounding of the fifth trumpet, John saw the image of a fallen angel who was given a key to open the bottomless pit. When it was opened, the smoke that arose from it saturated the air, masking the light from the sun and moon. As swarms of what appeared to be locusts at first glance began to emerge from the pit, John noted that these deadly creatures were given authority to torment everyone on the earth except for the 144,000 servants who wore God's mark on their foreheads.

And they were not permitted to kill anyone, but to torment for five months; and their torment was like the torment of a scorpion when it stings a man. And in those days men will seek death and will not find it; they will long to die, and death flees from them.

9:5-6

Next, John described these winged creatures as having lion's teeth, and bodies that resembled horses but with human faces and scorpion-like tails. They wore iron breastplates and golden crowns atop their long, flowing hair. As they flew, John likened the sound of the swarm to that of many horses carrying soldiers to battle. This event is referred to as the first of three "woes."

The next trumpet sound came from the sixth angel, who was instructed to release four fallen angels who had been imprisoned beneath the river Euphrates in preparation for this very hour. In this next image, the fallen angels were given authority to kill a third of mankind with the plagues of fire, smoke, and brimstone that were brought on by two hundred million armies of demons on horseback. John described the appearance of these demons as well.

And this is how I saw in my vision the horses and those who sat on them: the riders had breastplates the color of fire, of hyacinth, and of brimstone; and the heads of the horses are like the heads of lions; and out of their mouths came fire and smoke and brimstone.

9:17

Nearing the end of the chapter, John was informed that the remainder of those on the earth who survive the first woe and are among the two-thirds not killed by the demons will remain unrepentant. As we learned already, those who are given white robes will indeed repent. And before the end of the book, we'll see that they will be killed by a means other than what John has seen thus far.

The rest of mankind, who were not killed by these plagues, did not repent of the works of their hands, so as not to worship demons, and the idols of gold and of silver and of brass and of stone and of wood, which can neither see nor hear nor walk; and they did not repent of their murders nor of their sorceries nor of their immorality nor of their thefts.

9:20-21

CHAPTER 10

In this next portion of the youngest disciple's vision, John is shown an image of a mighty angel whose features were similar to those of Jesus when he appeared on Patmos. This angel was gigantic in size, having one foot in the sea and the other on the land.

I saw another strong angel coming down out of heaven, clothed with a cloud; and the rainbow was upon his head, and his face was like the sun, and his feet like pillars of fire; and he had in his hand a little book which was open.

10:1-2

And when the giant angel cried out with a voice like a roaring lion, seven peals of thunder began to speak. As for what they said, this will remain a mystery as John was ordered to stop writing and to keep their words a secret.

When the seven peals of thunder had spoken, I was about to write; and I heard a voice from heaven saying, "Seal up the things which the seven peals of thunder have spoken and do not write them."

10:4

With his right hand lifted toward heaven, the angel appealed to God the Father and declared that there would be no more delay. As the angel's voice continued to ring out, he advised that the seventh trumpet would bring an end to all things, just as God had assured His servants and His prophets. John then heard the same voice that instructed him not to write down the words of the seven thunders. This time, the voice called for John to interact with the images he was seeing.

Then the voice which I heard from heaven, I heard again speaking with me, and saying, "Go, take the book which is open in the hand of the angel who stands on the sea and on the land."

10:8

As John approached and requested the book, the angel instructed him to eat it, assuring him that the book would taste sweet but would sour his stomach. And so, John retrieved the book and ate it, confirming how sweet it tasted and how bad it made his stomach feel. Lastly, John was told that he would need to prophesy again before people of many nations and their kings, presumably after being released from the confines of Patmos.

REVELATION 11 & 12

The life, death, and resurrection of the two witnesses.

CHAPTER 11

As John's written record continues, he recalled being given a measuring rod and an instruction to measure the holy temple, but only the area that will be used for worship and for sacrificial offerings. The portion he was told to exclude (the courtyard) will be occupied by people who will come to Jerusalem from all over the world during a period of 42 months. The significance of the measuring rod could indicate that John saw the temple as it was being built. And those confined to the courtyard might be builders or even tourists who come from all over to see the temple's construction.

Leave out the courtyard which is outside the temple and do not measure it, because it has been given to the nations; and they will trample the holy city for forty-two months.

11:2

Next, John was informed that God's two witnesses will preach the gospel for 1,260 days. Because these periods of 42 months and 1,260 days are equal, we may conclude that the people from other nations and these two mystery men will be present in Jerusalem at the same time. Referred to as "olive trees," the two witnesses may be who Zechariah encountered in his own vision (Zech 4:11-14). They may also have ministered to Jesus during the event we call *the transfiguration*. Hear me out on this one.

Earlier, I called your attention to the powers given to the two witnesses and how they might reveal their identities. Right away, we can pair Elijah with stopping the rain, as he did this before he died. And he did it for 42 months, just as he will do later. You can read about this in the 17th chapter of James' book. As for turning water into blood, Moses appears to be our top candidate for having stricken this very plague upon Egypt. There is, however, another power that neither of them will have used before. And it's awesome!

And if anyone wants to harm them, fire flows out of their mouth and devours their enemies; so if anyone wants to harm them, he must be killed in this way.
11:5

Continuing on, we learn that these two fire-breathing preachers will have gained worldwide attention before

God allows them to be killed by the Antichrist—but not before they complete their mission to lead 144,000 Jewish men and women to Jesus over the course of 1,260 days (three and a half years). And when they are killed, instead of being buried, the two men's bodies will be left in the streets of Jerusalem for the whole world to rejoice over. Much like Jesus' death, theirs will be short-lived.

But after three and a half days, the breath of life from God came into them, and they stood on their feet; and great fear fell upon those who were watching them. And they heard a loud voice from heaven saying to them, "Come up here." Then they went up into heaven in the cloud, and their enemies watched them.

11:11-12

On this same day, after the two men ascend into heaven, John tells us that an earthquake will cause a tenth of the city to become a giant sinkhole. This is the bottomless pit that the demon locusts swarmed out of in an image he described earlier. And we're told that 7,000 people will perish during this incident. Given all that Ezekiel told us about this day, those 7,000 may consist of the soldiers from the northern and southern armies, as the people from Israel will have fled to the mountains after the abomination showed up and killed the two witnesses three days earlier.

And that time, there was a great earthquake, and a tenth of the city fell. Seven thousand people were killed in the earthquake, and the rest were terrified and gave glory to the God of heaven.

11:13

Next, we're told that this day's events represent the conclusion of the second woe. Given that the two witnesses will awaken less than four days after their second lifespan of 1,260 days, we know that this woe will conclude on day 1,263, which is just past the midpoint of the seven years. And it is around this time that we as God's church can expect to make our grand exit. Moving on, John then described hearing the seventh and final trumpet and how it sparked resounding praises within the throne room, beginning with a hymn that I wouldn't mind hearing more often than just at Christmas time.

"The kingdom of the world has become the kingdom of our Lord and of His Christ; and He will reign forever and ever."

11:15

After this, John watched as another earthquake, this time with planet-shaking magnitude, along with a storm of giant hailstones, destroyed the earth and all who remained on it. This marks the 2,550th day—our earth's last. Once again, I'd like to reiterate that John was not witnessing these actual events unfold, but was being shown how they will play out in the future. Soon, Revelation will take us back through these years again to zoom in even further on the conflict involving the false prophet and the Antichrist as a beast.

CHAPTER 12

So far, the images John saw in this vision had largely informed him about the future. In this chapter, we see them being used to tell him about the past in the form of a mini drama, complete with its own cast of characters.

THE WOMAN

Here, God assigned the female persona to the land of Israel, clothed with the sun and wearing a crown of 12 stars, which is believed to represent its 12 tribes. In this segment, John saw that this "woman" was in labor and about to give birth.

THE RED DRAGON

Next, we're introduced to a dragon (Satan) whose tail swept up a third of the stars in the sky and threw them down on the earth. This dragon was seen standing before the woman, eagerly waiting for her to give birth so that he might devour the child.

THE MALE CHILD

When the baby was delivered, John saw that this was no ordinary child.

And she gave birth to a son, a male child, who is to rule all the nations with a rod of iron; and her child was caught up to God and to His throne.

12:5

John then saw the mother of the child (Israel) flee to the mountains, where God will keep His chosen people safe during the second half of the seven years that are to come. This is in line with Jesus' instruction to Israel, as found in three of the four Gospels.

THE ANGEL

In this scene, John watched as the angel Michael engaged and overpowered Satan and his angel followers in the battle that took place between the days of creation and Eve's temptation. He even got to see a depiction how this battle ended.

And the great dragon was thrown down, the serpent of old who is called the devil and Satan, who deceives the whole world; he was thrown down to the earth, and his angels were thrown down with him.

12:9

Chapter 12 comes to a close after a brief recap of the events that make up this drama. To offer my own recap, John essentially watched Satan's failed attempts to conquer heaven and rid the world of Jesus. In an after-credits scene, Satan gave up and began to focus his attention on increasing the number of people who will be given white robes.

REVELATION 13 & 14

A harvest brings the Antichrist's reign to an end.

CHAPTER 13

The book of Daniel informs us that it will be the Antichrist as a man who will kill the two witnesses and then be killed himself shortly after. Chapter 13 opens with an image of the Antichrist as a beast, who is Satan (the dragon) disguised as the deceased king, complete with scars to deceive the world into believing he was resurrected. While we do read about angels appearing in human form throughout the Bible, whatever transpires here will be enabled by God in order to achieve His will during this time.

I saw one of his heads as if it had been slain, and his fatal wound was healed. And the whole earth was amazed and followed after the beast; they worshiped the dragon because he gave his authority to the beast; and they worshiped the beast, saying, "Who is like the beast, and who is able to wage war with him?"

13:3-4

In the verse we just read, the dragon (Satan) giving his "authority" suggests that he will have control over the beast, which is the Antichrist (the likeness of the deceased king). And Satan will prompt the beast to blaspheme God and begin killing those who are led to Christ by the newly converted 144,000 Jewish ministers during the 42-month period following the rapture.

It was also given to him to make war with the saints and to overcome them, and authority over every tribe and people and tongue and nation was given to him. All who dwell on the earth will worship him, everyone whose name has not been written from the foundation of the world in the book of life of the Lamb who has been slain.

13:7-8

Next, we are introduced to a second beast, which is the false prophet. Having been left behind by the rapture, this man's role will be to persuade the people on the earth to worship and submit to the first beast, which is the Antichrist.

He exercises all the authority of the first beast in his presence. And he makes the earth and those who dwell in it to worship the first beast, whose fatal wound was healed.

13:12

Serving as the Antichrist's spokesperson, the false prophet will perform "signs and wonders," including calling fire down from heaven, to convince people to fall in line. With the rapture having left the world in a broken state, this man will pledge security to those who will receive the Antichrist's mark on their hand or forehead. To those who flee and do not receive the mark, the false prophet will call for their deaths.

Finally, we are informed that the beast's mark, 666, is somehow tied to the king whose likeness Satan will use to deceive the world. And those with wisdom are invited to a challenge that involves the calculation of this number, as we discussed previously.

CHAPTER 14

This chapter opens with John describing an image of Mt. Zion, which lies just south of the walled city of Jerusalem. On this mountain was Jesus, along with the chosen 144,000 who bore God's name on their foreheads. John then heard a loud voice from heaven that sounded to him like harpists playing their instruments. This voice was singing a song that only the 144,000 could understand. John then saw an angel flying above the mountain who possessed an "eternal gospel" and gave a warning to the people on the earth who were from every nation.

And he said with a loud voice, "Fear God, and give Him glory, because the hour of His judgment has come; worship Him who made the heaven and the earth and sea and springs of waters."

14:7

Another angel announced the destruction of "Babylon the great," which is an entity of great significance that we'll learn more about in chapter 17. Its crimes included influencing the world with immorality, according to the angel. Following was a third angel who had yet another warning for the people on the earth.

If anyone worships the beast and his image, and receives a mark on his forehead or on his hand, he also will drink of the wine of the wrath of God, which is mixed in full strength in the cup of His anger; and he will be tormented with fire and brimstone in the presence of the holy angels and in the presence of the Lamb.

14:9-10

Next, John described seeing one who was "like a son of man" (a reference that points to Jesus) on top of a cloud wearing a golden crown. When an angel stepped forward and announced that the earth's harvest was ripe for reaping, Jesus swung a sickle over the earth and gathered what many believe is the remainder of those who were still alive and who had repented of their sins. Often confused with the rapture, this event is foreshadowed in the books of Luke and Matthew, where one of two men and two women is taken, leaving the other behind (Matt. 24:40-41, Luke 17:35-27).

Finally, with the harvesting having been completed, John watched as an angel announced that it was time to gather the remaining clusters of grapes (those who remained unrepentant). This time, an angel swung a sickle and tossed all who were gathered into a winepress (the wrath of God) from which blood flowed and flooded the earth over a 200-mile radius. While the sickle and winepress in this image are allegorical, the melting of the giant hailstones that lend themselves to this destruction could produce what we see in this last verse if the flooding in the image foreshadows a real-world event.

They were trampled in the winepress outside the city, and blood flowed out of the press, rising as high as the horses' bridles for a distance of 1,600 stadia.
14:20

REVELATION 15 & 16
Plagues are revisited as golden bowls are poured.

CHAPTER 15

Then I saw another sign in heaven, great and marvelous, seven angels who had seven plagues, which are the last, because in them the wrath of God is finished.

15:1

This relatively short 15th chapter of Revelation serves as a prelude to the events in chapter 16. Here, John saw golden bowls being distributed among seven angels, much like he did when the seven trumpets were handed out. These golden bowls were filled with God's wrath and were about to be poured down on the earth resulting in a plague. And each bowl coincided with the plagues that were triggered by the sounding of each of the seven trumpets. So, a trumpet sounded, a bowl was poured, and a plague... plagued, I guess.

And one of the four living creatures gave the seven angels seven golden bowls full of the wrath of God, who lives forever and ever. And the temple was filled with smoke from the glory of God and from His power; and no one was able to enter the temple until the seven plagues of the seven angels were finished.

15:7-8

CHAPTER 16

As with previous chapters, this one depicts John being provided with a new level of zoom that revealed even more details of these familiar events. While John chose to group his descriptions according to what triggered these images inside the throne room (broken seals, trumpets, golden bowls, etc.), these events may or may not have been shown to John in this order. As confusing as his written portrayal can be, we must remind ourselves that this was all a vision and nothing needed to be done a certain way, despite our feelings to the contrary. I certainly would have presented things differently. But, alas, I wasn't there. And neither was John.

As chapter 16 begins, a loud voice from within the temple in heaven instructed the angels who had been given golden bowls of wrath to begin pouring them out upon the earth, one by one.

So the first angel went and poured out his bowl on the earth; and it became a loathsome and malignant sore on the people who had the mark of the beast and who worshiped his image.

16:2

Mirroring the events within the images that appeared when the second and third trumpets were blown, the pouring of the second and third bowls of wrath resulted in the sea turning to blood and the poisoning of the rivers and streams respectively. And like the fourth trumpet, we see how the plague from the fourth golden bowl involves the sun.

The fourth angel poured out his bowl upon the sun, and it was given to it to scorch men with fire. Men were scorched with fierce heat; and they blasphemed the name of God who has the power over these plagues, and they did not repent so as to give Him glory.

16:8-9

As for the fifth bowl, its plague included the infliction of immense pain and sores that may have been the result of the flying locust/demons who stung like scorpions after the fifth trumpet sounded. The sixth bowl also followed this pattern, causing the Euphrates River to dry up.

While the sixth trumpet involved releasing fallen angels from beneath the Euphrates, the coinciding bowl of wrath was to make way for armies from the east to assemble in northern Israel for the Battle of Armageddon. And they'll need to cross that river to get there.

And they gathered them together to the place which in Hebrew is called Har-Magedon.

16:16

Just as the seventh trumpet was to bring an end to all things, the pouring of the seventh and final bowl was preceded by a loud voice from within God's temple saying, "It is done." Because we've already learned about this final event, we might expect to hear about those hailstones again. And here they are.

Every island fled away and the mountains could not be found. From the sky huge hailstones, each weighing about a hundred pounds, fell on people. And they cursed God on account of the plague of hail, because the plague was so terrible.

16:20-21

REVELATION 17 & 18

A city is destroyed for having led the world astray.

CHAPTER 17

In the opening scene of chapter 17, one of the angels who poured out a golden bowl approached John and invited him to see the judgment of the "MOTHER OF HARLOTS"—aka 'Babylon the great.'

Come here, I will show you the judgment of the great harlot who sits on many waters, with whom the kings of the earth committed acts of immorality, and those who dwell on the earth were made drunk with the wine of her immorality.

17:1-2

If we skip ahead to the last verse in this chapter, we learn that this "harlot" is not a person, but a city that God is likening to Babylon. This is consistent with the Bible's frequent use of the female persona when referring to nations and cities.

While John may have been confused until he learned this, you and I can know this up front and begin putting the pieces together, starting with the city's association with red and purple clothing and structures adorned with precious jewels. And its crimes of killing Jesus' disciples assure us that this city existed in Jesus' day and continues to operate at the time of the end.

The woman was clothed in purple and scarlet, and adorned with gold and precious stones and pearls, having in her hand a gold cup full of abominations and of the unclean things of her immorality. And I saw the woman drunk with the blood of the saints, and with the blood of the witnesses of Jesus.

17:4, 6

Here, John was shown a view of a city that the angel explained had been "riding the beast." And the word *beast* here is given a double meaning. Not only is the city following after the Antichrist (riding the beast), it also *sits* upon a beast with seven heads. And these seven heads, according to the angel, refer to seven prominent hills that mark the city's geographical location.

This calls for a mind with wisdom. The seven heads are seven hills on which the woman sits.

17:9

Next, the angel describes the Antichrist as being an "eighth king" (8th to rule over his nation) and also a member of the group of seven kings that we analyzed earlier. As for the ten horns, they are a group of individuals who will swear allegiance to the Antichrist. These are said to possess the sole purpose of doing the Antichrist's bidding in exchange for positions of power. But that power doesn't last.

These will wage war against the Lamb, and the Lamb will overcome them because He is Lord of lords and King of kings; and those who are with Him are the called and chosen and faithful.

17:14

As the chapter comes to a close, the angel explained to John that the city has influence over multitudes of people from every nation. The angel also spoke of the city's relationship with world leaders by telling John that it exercises authority apart from the kings of the earth. It's also noteworthy that this city is called an "apostasy" in 2 Thessalonians. This word refers to the abandonment of sound biblical doctrine in favor of that which is unsound or unbiblical. Coupled with its history of Christian martyrdom and worldwide influence, this city is widely understood to serve as the headquarters of a religious institution or church where the false prophet will have a prominent role.

CHAPTER 18

As the angel shows John this city that serves as the object of God's scorn, another angel was seen descending from heaven, declaring the city's destruction. In a loud voice, the angel labeled the city a "dwelling place of demons" and a "prison of every unclean spirit" for having led people from every nation of the world astray with a gospel that is different from what the disciples learned from Jesus.

For her sins have piled up as high as heaven, and God has remembered her iniquities.

18:5

This voice from heaven also described how this institution will be punished to the same degree that it has glorified itself like an evil queen who considers it beneath her to have ever been married to a king. As we read on, we learn that this city also utilizes a shipping port whose merchants will mourn the city's burning as they'll no longer have a place to sell their precious cargo.

And the merchants of the earth weep and mourn over her, because no one buys their cargoes any more—cargoes of gold and silver and precious stones and pearls and fine linen of purple and scarlet, and every kind of citron wood and every article of ivory and

every article made from very costly wood and bronze and iron and marble, and cinnamon and spice and incense and perfume and frankincense and wine and olive oil...

18:11-13

Chapter 18 ends with a call to rejoice over the city's destruction. And that celebration continues into chapter 19.

All the nations were deceived by her sorcery. And in her was found the blood of prophets and of saints and of all who have been slain on the earth.

18:23-24

Here's a quick recap before we continue. The Bible's label of "great harlot" belongs to a city whose location features seven prominent hills or mountains. Operating as the headquarters of a worldwide church or denomination, it may be recognized for its palatial structures decorated with precious jewels and costly materials, which it receives from merchants who travel by boat to its shipping port. Fine red and purple garments are also noteworthy among its imports. While the attitude this city possesses in relation to other churches may be tough to detect, its authority apart from world leaders and its history of Christian martyrdom are very public matters.

One more quick thought. I refuse to believe that God's purpose for providing this information is to bring about doubt or a hesitancy to recognize the forest for the trees. While God didn't name this city outright, He essentially placed His finger on the map. You likely know which city this is. If you don't, a quick Google search with these details will reveal it, along with the multitudes of people all over the world who are being led astray by its false teaching. Pray for them. Pray for an opportunity to minister to them yourself. This is not something we need to ignore or be in denial about.

If this is your church, do not pretend that God is not speaking to you. I recognize that the thought of leaving this church may be devastating, especially if you've been a part of it your whole life. But if this is how God wants to receive you, by all means, surrender. Run to Him as fast as you can! Institutions formed by flawed human beings have only divided us. Our loyalty belongs to God, not a denomination.

The last verse we'll look at regarding this city actually appears earlier in the chapter. But it may be the most important one in all of Revelation.

Come out of her, my people, so that you will not participate in her sins and receive of her plagues.
18:4

REVELATION 19 & 20

A new earth follows Jesus' victory at Armageddon.

CHAPTER 19

At the beginning of this chapter, the celebration over the destruction of the "mother of harlots" breaks out with a multitude of praises in heaven.

Hallelujah! Salvation and glory and power belong to our God; because His judgments are true and righteous; for He has judged the great harlot who was corrupting the earth with her immorality, and He has avenged the blood of His bondservants on her.

19:1-2

Next, John's angel informed him that it was time to rejoice over the marriage supper of the lamb, which is the union of Jesus and the raptured church whose members are named in the book of life. While the rapture event is not mentioned here, this verse is the very first indicator that it had taken place.

As John became overwhelmed and fell at the angel's feet in worship, he was ordered to cease and desist.

Then I fell at his feet to worship him. But he said to me, "Do not do that; I am a fellow servant of yours and your brothers and sisters who hold the testimony of Jesus; worship God!"

19:10

The next image John was shown was of Jesus and the raptured saints emerging from the cloud, all riding white horses. This is the cloud that both the dead in Christ and the saints living on the earth will ascend to on our day of redemption. Jesus, who was prepared for battle, was described as having eyes like fire and wearing many crowns along with a white robe dipped in blood. As for the saints, their garments were all white and clean. This time, instead of referring to Jesus as "like a son of man," John wrote down his name, which is "The Word of God."

From His mouth comes a sharp sword, so that with it He may strike down the nations, and He will rule them with a rod of iron; and He treads the wine press of the fierce wrath of God, the Almighty. And on His robe and on His thigh He has a name written, KING OF KINGS, AND LORD OF LORDS.

19:15-16

John then described seeing all of the armies that had gathered to destroy Jesus in this battle at Armageddon. He also saw an angel call out to the birds in the air, instructing them to prepare to feast on the bodies of every class of human being that was about to fall. Before decimating these military forces, Jesus tossed both the Antichrist and the false prophet into the giant pit that opened during the first earthquake—a pit that will lead to the fires of hell beneath the surface of our earth. Victory in Jesus!!!

CHAPTER 20

John's vision now shifts to inform him of life on a new earth, where Satan will be allowed to roam after being bound for a thousand years in hell.

And he threw him [Satan] into the abyss, and shut it and sealed it over him, so that he would not deceive the nations any longer, until the thousand years were completed; after these things he must be released for a short time.

20:3

With Satan out of the picture temporarily, John's attention was directed to an image of the tribulation saints in white robes who will refuse the Antichrist's mark and repent of their sins. Here we are told how they will be killed for their testimonies.

And I saw the souls of those who had been beheaded because of their testimony of Jesus and because of the word of God, and those who had not worshiped the beast or his image, and had not received the mark on their forehead and on their hand; and they came to life and reigned with Christ for a thousand years.

20:4

These he watched "come to life" and begin to live out their thousand years on the new earth where Jesus would also be. This was called the "first resurrection." The rest of the dead, which consists of everyone who has ever died without having placed their trust in Jesus, would also come to life, but not until after the thousand years are complete. This awakening of the dead will be to face judgment.

As we read on, we learn of a great city on the new earth called "New Jerusalem" that raptured saints will inherit. The tribulation saints will not be allowed to enter the city, as their names will not be written in the book of life. And we are told that the purpose of Satan's release toward the end of the thousand years will be to tempt them one last time. This temptation appears to involve the same tactic that Satan used in the Garden of Eden. Targeting their envy and jealousy, Satan will influence them to believe that they deserve what they have been denied.

And they came up on the broad plain of the earth and surrounded the camp of the saints and the beloved city, and fire came down from heaven and devoured them.

20:9

After seeing how God will destroy all those who will be gifted white robes and a thousand additional years of life, John watched as Satan was tossed back into the depths of hell. This time, he would be bound and tortured for all eternity. As we approach the end of this chapter, we see that John was shown an ominous location that had been separated from both heaven and the new earth. Here, he saw the arrival of every unsaved soul who had died since time began, including all who resided outside the great city on the new earth. As books were opened that revealed all they had done, each was judged accordingly. While their deeds varied from soul to soul, their punishment was equal and just.

This is the second death, the lake of fire. And if anyone's name was not found written in the book of life, he was thrown into the lake of fire.

20:14-15

REVELATION 21 & 22

John sees the great city and Jesus gives a wake-up call.

CHAPTER 21

After being informed of how life on the new earth will play out among those without access to the great city, John's vision shifts back to the very beginning of the thousand years. Here, the zoom lens is now centered on those who will live *within* the city and who God Himself will dwell among. These will no longer experience death nor the pain and suffering associated with life in human bodies.

Then I saw a new heaven and a new earth; for the first heaven and the first earth passed away, and there is no longer any sea. And I saw the holy city, new Jerusalem, coming down out of heaven from God, prepared as a bride adorned for her husband. And I heard a loud voice from the throne saying, "Look! God's dwelling place is now among the people, and he will dwell with them.

21:1-3

After seeing an image of this gigantic city as it was seated upon the new earth, John heard God speak from the throne as He presented a contrast between the groups who will inhabit the new earth. Some will have eternal access to the water of life (raptured saints), while others who continue to give in to their sinful nature (tribulation saints) will be destined for eternal punishment, which is called the "second death."

While examining the appearance of this great city, John noted that it had 12 gates—three on each wall, which were named for the 12 sons of the tribes of Israel, and also 12 foundation stones, each named for one of the twelve Apostles. These two groups of men are believed to have been represented by the 24 elders John saw seated to the left and right of God's throne.

The city is laid out as a square, and its length is as great as the width; and he [the angel] measured the city with the rod, fifteen hundred miles; its length and width and height are equal. And he measured its wall, seventy-two yards, according to human measurements, which are also angelic measurements.

21:16-17

According to the angel's measurements, each wall was roughly 24 times the height of our earth's atmosphere, which rises 62 miles from the earth's surface. And the thickness of each wall will be like the wingspan of a 747 jet. So, if this city fits snuggly within these walls, the area it will occupy on the new earth will be akin to all 50 of our United States combined. This is going to be one BIG city!

The material of the wall was jasper; and the city was pure gold, like clear glass. The foundation stones of the city wall were decorated with every kind of precious stone.

21:18-19

After describing the appearance of the materials that made up the walls and the city itself, John noted that there was no temple to be found within the city walls, as God and His son served as the temple. There was also no light from a sun or moon, nor was it needed, as God had illuminated the city and the surrounding nations with the radiance of His son, Jesus. Lastly, after being told that the city gates would always be open, a description of those who were not allowed to enter the city was reiterated to John.

And nothing unclean, and no one who practices abomination and lying, shall ever come into it, but only those whose names are written in the Lamb's book of life.

21:27

CHAPTER 22

At the beginning of chapter 21, John wrote that there was no ocean or sea to be seen on the new earth. In this final chapter, John's vision affirms that there will indeed be a body of water in the form of a river that flows from God's throne. This is referred to as the "river of life." Being that the tribulation saints will be led to drink from it (Rev. 7:16), we may conclude that this river extends beyond the city walls and winds over the surface of the new earth.

And he showed me a river of the water of life, clear as crystal, coming from the throne of God and of the Lamb.

22:1

Next, John was shown trees along the riverbank that will produce twelve kinds of fruit and whose leaves were for "the healing of the nations."

There will no longer be any curse; and the throne of God and of the Lamb will be in it, and His bond-servants will serve Him; they will see His face, and His name will be on their foreheads.

22:3-4

After explaining how the illumination of Christ will eliminate night on the new earth, the angel then informed John of the words Jesus spoke to the prophets and how they were faithful and true. These words include the blessing that was presented at the beginning of Revelation.

And behold, I am coming quickly. Blessed is he who heeds the words of the prophecy of this book.

22:7

Beginning with verse 8, the shift in John's narrative suggests that his vision had come to a conclusion. Now seemingly awake on Patmos and with Jesus still in the room with him, John addressed all those who will be reading the words that he wrote, providing us with the assurance that he did indeed see and hear all that experienced during his vision. He even attested to falling at the angel's feet in worship when his vision became overwhelming. John then continued his conversation with Jesus, whose words fill the remainder of the verses in Revelation.

And he said to me, "Do not seal up the words of the prophecy of this book, for the time is near. Let the one who does wrong still do wrong, and the one who is filthy still be filthy; and let the one who is righteous still practice righteousness, and the one who is holy still keep himself holy."

22:10-11

Addressing himself as the "Alpha & Omega" who is coming quickly, Jesus spoke of his reward (the great city) that he will bring with him and contrasted those who will receive his reward with those who will be denied access to the city.

"Blessed are those who wash their robes, so that they will have the right to the tree of life, and may enter the city by the gates. Outside are the dogs, the sorcerers, the sexually immoral persons, the murderers, the idolaters, and everyone who loves and practices lying."

22:14-15

Before concluding with a message of hope, Jesus addressed all who would add their own words to this book and how they will be subject to the plagues which are written in it. Taking words away from the book, according to Jesus, would also be punished severely. Much like those who remain in the great harlot, offenders will be denied the reward of spending eternity with him inside the great city. And now, the final words in our Holy Bible.

He who testifies to these things says, "Yes, I am coming quickly." Amen. Come, Lord Jesus. The grace of the Lord Jesus be with all. Amen.

22:20-21

REFLECTION

Revisiting the declaration at the beginning and end of this amazing book, God assures us that we who trust in Jesus have the capacity to read, understand, and react to this text in obedience. Sadly, far too many men and women have surrendered to the idea that we don't. Arguments to support this notion include Revelation being purposefully cryptic or intended only for those with ultra wisdom-validating credentials to make sense of it all. But doesn't the same Spirit who speaks to them also speak to you and me?

The way I see it, the extent of one's wisdom has never been limited by the absence of a seminary education. This wisdom doesn't even come from the world. God gives it to all who ask for it, provided we use it to glorify Him. Even so, wisdom of any amount doesn't change the fact that we're all humans with imperfect ways of thinking. Thankfully, the Bible is *always* on point. It may not tell us everything, but we can trust that it was designed entirely for our understanding, despite our inability to understand it entirely.

Regarding our reaction to Revelation in obedience, this may also be understood by diving into the preceding books of the Bible. Here are some verses that demonstrate this.

Beloved, do not believe every spirit, but test the spirits to see whether they are from God, for many false prophets have gone out into the world.

1 John 4:1

For whatever was written in former days was written for our instruction.

Romans 15:4

Now when these things begin to take place, straighten up and raise your heads, because your redemption is drawing near.

Luke 21:28

And do this, understanding the present time: The hour has already come for you to wake up from your slumber, because our salvation is nearer now than when we first believed.

Romans 13:11

So be on your guard; I have told you everything ahead of time.

Mark 13:23

Despite being found in five different places within the Bible, these verses read as if they were spoken in a single conversation. I wasn't actually trying to achieve this. But it's often the outcome when people gather supporting verses of Scripture. It's kind of like those music mash-ups featuring multiple songs that blend together beautifully. Lyrically, however, these mash-ups can be a real mess, whereas God's Word is seamless.

So, if you haven't detected it already, there's a huge push for the readiness of God's church in the Bible. And those who are ready can recognize where we are on the timeline based on the many things the Scriptures call to our attention. While my goal for this book did not include pointing out fulfilled end-times prophecies, I made a valiant effort to present some very specific events in my other book that either occurred during our generation or are currently unfolding just as the Bible says they will. These are among the many things that Jesus commanded us to be aware of. And yet, I recall being made to feel like a heretic for pointing them out by voices who insisted that Jesus could return a hundred years from now, and it could still be called "soon."

Apparently, there's a feeling of comfort in adopting this attitude. And it translates to "Me now. Jesus later." Recalling the parable of ten virgins in Matthew's book, the text paints a picture of a group of young ladies who set out in the darkness of night to meet their bridegroom. This was a day they were told to prepare for their entire lives. And being prepared for this meeting included carrying a lamp so that they would be recognized in the darkness. While each of the ten ladies felt that they were fully prepared, only five of them actually were. And so, when it was announced that the bridegroom was approaching, the unprepared ladies realized that their lamps did not have enough oil to stay lit any longer.

So, after their pleas to borrow oil from the other five were met with a big "no," they quickly left the scene to have their lamps refilled. And it was while they were gone that the bridegroom arrived and gathered the five whose lamps were lit to attend a wedding feast. When the five ladies who left the group finally returned, they were devastated not only to find the other five gone, but that they had been locked out of the hall where the feast had been prepared. And their cries to the bridegroom to be let inside were met with the same reply Jesus said he will give to those who will feel certain that they are Christians at the time of the rapture, but are not.

And then I will declare to them, 'I never knew you.'
Matthew 7:23

Let me be perfectly clear. Missing some of the details or being confused about the end times has no impact on one's salvation. On the new earth, we will live and worship alongside people who had no clue when the rapture was going to happen. In fact, their readiness will not have taken the rapture or any of the signs and signals of the end times into account at all. Jesus is who they will have made themselves ready for. And he extended his wedding invitation to us all ages ago when he was crucified on our behalf. And yet, many feel like they can cram for Jesus at the last minute, the way many of us have done for exams. This, my friends, is not what a courtship is. If we can put Jesus off, it's only because we possess no love for him. And that love cannot be obtained hastily in fear of having no time left to obtain it.

Throughout the Bible, we are assured that knowing Jesus intimately and trusting in him are the essential ingredients for salvation. We can tie his name to our identities, but we can't truly love him if we don't know him. And it would be impossible to have ever worshiped him if we don't love him. While I'm ecstatic that you've chosen to join me for this awesome journey through Revelation, I implore you, once again, not to allow your motive for exploring God's Word to be anything other than a means to draw closer and closer to our Lord and Savior.

While there is indeed an end to this earth in the works, there's no window of time we should feel bound by as we seek this relationship. Jesus will not be leaving the big screen the way movies do. So, sit back, relax, and take in his amazing love. Relish every moment and let the truth whisk you away into God's presence as it did for John. While I've certainly felt the urge to proclaim that our time on earth is running out, I rest knowing that Jesus is already on top of this. And if his words aren't enough to wake people up, those written by some Bible nerd from Tennessee will have no effect. But I can definitely stir up excitement over what's to come, knowing that we need only to keep our lamps burning a little longer before our bridegroom carries us away to our wedding feast. Until that day comes, stand strong and don't worry. If your heart burns for Jesus, your lamp will always have plenty of oil.

Till next time!

www.ingramcontent.com/pod-product-compliance
Lightning Source LLC
LaVergne TN
LVHW041627070426
835507LV00008B/494